7 48 49 50 51 52 1 2 3 4 5 6

fifty–two

OPENING TALKS FOR CHILDREN

Eileen M. Ritter

CPH
SAINT LOUIS

Contents

The Commandments

Someone's Coming!
Waiting for God's Promises to Come True

Bible References: Jer. 23:5–6, Deut. 18:15, Ps. 110:4.

Materials: Paper crown, cardboard sword, scroll (length of shelf paper glued to two wooden dowels or pencils), paper sign with the word *Priest* (attach a piece of string to each end so sign can be hung around a child's neck), baby doll, Bible with verses for this lesson marked.

Before you begin: Call four children to help you. Choose a fifth child who is a good reader to read the marked Bible texts.

Can you remember a promise that someone made to you? Did you think about the promise often? Was it hard to wait until the promised words came true?

Long ago God talked to His people through people called prophets. Through these prophets God made promises to His people. He told them He was going to send a Messiah.

God's people remembered His promises. They thought about them often. They waited and waited for the promised words to come true.

In the Bible we can read God's promises about the Messiah He would send . Listen to one of the promises God gave through His prophet, Jeremiah. *Ask the reader to read Jer. 23:5–6.*

When God's people heard Jeremiah's words, they were very excited. "A king!" they said. "Just like our father, David." *Place crown on first child's head.* "A soldier!" said others. "He'll fight for us against our enemies." *Give sword to second child.*

Moses told the people another of God's promises. *Have the reader read Deut. 18:15.* "Yes, we understand," said the people, "the Messiah will be a prophet. We will listen to everything He says." *Give scroll to the third child.*

Another of God's promises is in the book of Psalms. *Ask the reader to read Ps. 110:4.* "He'll be a priest," the people said. "He'll sacrifice animals to pay for our sins." *Place "Priest" sign around fourth child's neck.*

Finally God kept His promises. In a little stable in Bethlehem, He sent just what He had promised—a baby boy. *Show doll.* "A baby?" the people wondered. "This can't be what God promised."

But the baby, who was God's own Son, was exactly what God promised. He came to be a king who would rule our hearts in love. He came to be a strong soldier, one who would fight for us against sin and the devil. He came to be a prophet, too, who would teach us about God and His wonderful plan to save us. And He came to be a very special priest—not one who would sacrifice animals for us, but one who would die on the cross Himself to be the sacrifice for our sins. Because His Son died for us, we can be God's children now on earth and forever in heaven. All God's promises about the Messiah came true in Baby Jesus.

Someone's Coming!
Getting Ready for the Guest

Bible Reference: Luke 3:1–18.

Materials: A small chalkboard, heavily smudged with chalk and covered with drawings—a child's slate would be perfect; a dry cloth and a wet cloth.

When Adam and Eve first sinned against God, He promised to send a Savior. Through His prophets God gave more promises about the Savior He would send.

For thousands of years God's people waited for Him to keep His promises. Finally the time came for God's promised words to come true. It was time for God's Son, the Savior, to be born.

To help the people get ready for the Savior who was to come, God sent John the Baptist. John wore clothes made of camel's hair. He preached out in the desert. Many people who heard him thought he was the one God had promised. But John told them that he had only been sent to prepare the way for the Messiah who was to come. How should they prepare for this special person?

Think about a time when someone special was coming to visit at your house. How did you prepare? *Let children respond.* Perhaps you helped dust the furniture and vacuum the rug. Maybe someone washed the windows and scrubbed the kitchen floor. Your family made your house as clean as possible for the one who was coming.

To help the people prepare for the Messiah God would send, John told them, "Repent and be baptized for the forgiveness of your sins." He wanted them to clean up their lives by being sorry for their sins. He wanted them to stop living the old, dirty, sinful way and begin to live the way God wanted them to live. John baptized many people. Then they were ready to listen to the Savior who was coming.

As we get ready to celebrate Christmas, we try to clean up our lives and get our hearts ready for Jesus. *Hold up the dirty chalkboard. Ask a child to clean the board with the dry cloth.* But cleaning our lives by ourselves can never get rid of all the dirt of sin.

We remember John's word: *Repent.* When we repent, we tell Jesus we are sorry that we have sinned. We ask Him to take away our sins. *Wipe chalkboard with wet cloth, removing all smudges.* We know that Jesus died on the cross to take the punishment for all of our sins. God's Baptism washes us clean. We ask Him to help us live the way He wants us to live—to love and share with those around us, to obey our parents and teachers, and to share with everyone we know the news that Jesus has come to be our Savior.

What Shall We Name the Baby?

Bible Reference: Matt. 1:18–25.

Materials: A book of names and their meanings.

Have you ever thought about how important your name is? Names make us special and set us apart from everyone else around us.

Names can even tell about what they are naming. For instance, if you had a puppy who was brown all over, you might name him Brownie, but you would never call him Spot. You wouldn't call your furry yellow-striped cat Blackie or Rover, but you might decide to name her Tiger or Fluff.

Names for people sometimes tell something about them too. *Show the book of names and their meanings.* This book tells the meanings of many names. Most of the meanings are very old. They may or may not describe the person who has that name today.

For example, my first name is _____. According to this book, my name means (*read the meaning from the book*). Do you think my name tells something about me or not?

Look up the names of several children in the book. Read the meanings and discuss the appropriateness of their names.

When parents are expecting a new baby, they often use a book like this to choose the right name for the baby. They might look for a name whose meaning tells about a quality they would like their baby to have. Or they may decide to name the baby after a relative, a favorite Bible character, or someone they admire.

When Mary and Joseph were expecting their baby, they didn't have to talk about names. Mary might have thought about naming her baby Joseph Jr. after her husband. Perhaps relatives thought they should name the baby after one of their famous ancestors, like David or Isaac or even Abraham.

But Mary and Joseph knew something special about their baby. The angel had told Mary that He would be the baby God had promised to send. God's prophets had given this baby names hundreds of years before. Isaiah had said He would be called Immanuel—"God with us." Isaiah gave the baby other names too—Wonderful Counselor, Mighty God, Everlasting Father, Prince of Peace. These names told what Mary's Son would be like: He would be a great King, He would be the almighty God, He would always care for His people like a Father, and He would bring peace between people and God.

But Joseph knew that he and Mary didn't have to choose the baby's name after all. The angel who told Joseph in a dream about the baby told him the name God Himself had picked out. This name's meaning told exactly what the baby would do. When Mary's baby grew up, He died on the cross to pay for the sins of all people, even your sins and mine. And His name told the whole story.

Do you know the name the angel told Joseph to choose? Matthew wrote it in his Gospel: "She will give birth to a son, and you are to give Him the name Jesus, because He will save His people from their sins" (Matt. 1:21).

Don't You Wish He'd Come Again?
He Came, He Comes, He Is Coming Again

Bible Reference: Matt. 24:30–31.

Materials: A small Nativity set or picture of Jesus in the manger.

It's almost Christmas. On Christmas we celebrate the day that God's Son, Jesus, came to live on earth. *Show children the Nativity set.* Jesus was born in a little town called Bethlehem about 2,000 years ago, and His parents laid Him down to sleep in the manger of a stable because Bethlehem's only hotel was already full.

Don't you wish you could have been in Bethlehem that Christmas night? Just think of what you would have heard and seen: Cows and donkeys quietly eating in the barn, Mary humming a lullaby near the manger, angels singing "Glory to God in the highest," shepherds running to Bethlehem to see what the angels were talking about. *If time allows, ask children to suggest what they might have heard and seen.* And, best of all, the holy baby who was God's own Son, wrapped in swaddling clothes and sleeping in the straw.

It's almost Christmas—here, in the time and place where we live, too. And this same Jesus, God's Son, comes to us again. We can't see Him, like Mary and the shepherds did. But we know that He came to us in our Baptism, when water and His Word marked us as His children. He is with us right now, just as He promised He would be, our Friend when we are lonely, our Helper when things go wrong, and our Joy when we are sad. Because Jesus died for us, God forgives us for all the bad things we do, and His Holy Spirit helps us to live for Him. Even though we can't see Him, we can talk to Him when we pray—and listen to Him when we read and study His Word in the Bible.

It's almost Christmas. Don't you wish Jesus would come again, so we could see Him and talk to Him face to face?

Jesus promised that He would come again. When God's trumpet sounds at the end of time, Jesus will come back to earth. He will come to judge all people who have ever lived. He will take His children who believe in Him home to live with Him forever in heaven. Those who do not believe in Him will go to eternal death in hell.

Many people are frightened to think of Jesus coming again. But we know that when God looks at us, He sees that all our sins have been taken away by Jesus' own death on the cross. So we Christians wait for Jesus' coming the way a little child waits for her parents to come pick her up after a long day at the baby-sitter's. We will be so happy to see the one who loves us. And we look forward to going home to be with Him always.

No one knows when Jesus will come again. But He will come, just as He promised. Amen, come, Lord Jesus.

Straw for the Manger

Bible Reference: Luke 2:1–7.

Materials: A manger (or a wooden box filled with straw), extra straw.

Read Luke 2:1–7 aloud to the children. What a day that first Christmas must have been! Joseph and Mary, along with all the other travelers, arriving in Bethlehem for Caesar's census. A hotel crowded with people, too full for guests like the poor couple from Nazareth who arrived too late to get a room for the night. A stable full of animals, where Mary gave birth to her first baby, wrapped Him in cloths, and laid Him in a manger.

God had sent His own Son, Jesus, into the world so that all people who believe in Him would be saved from their sins. Jesus would grow up and show people, through His teaching and the loving things He did, what God is like. Then He would die on the cross in our place, to take the punishment we deserved for our sins. Because Jesus died for us, and rose again, we can be God's children here on earth and forever in heaven. We love Jesus because He did all this for us.

Show children the manger. I don't think a manger bed would be a very comfortable place to sleep, do you? If you were in Bethlehem on that first Christmas, you might have brought more straw to make the bed softer for the Baby you love so much. *Place another handful of straw in the manger.* What else could you have done for Baby Jesus to show you loved Him? *Allow the children to suggest things they might have done.*

Even though we love Jesus very much, we can't go back in time to Bethlehem to do these things for Him. But we can show our love for Him by loving those around us. When we share our food and clothing with the poor and homeless because of our love for Jesus, we are helping Him too. *Add straw to the manger.* It is as if we could add straw to His manger bed. When we obey our parents without grumbling, when we help our brothers and sisters without expecting them to help us in return, when we are friendly to the friendless or spend time with the old or the sick, we act out the love we feel in our hearts for the Baby in the stable. *Add straw.* And when we tell others about His birth like the shepherds did, we help them to feel Jesus' love for them too.

Grandpa's Friend

Bible Reference: Luke 2:25–38.

Materials: none.

"Good morning, Dad," said Tim as he plopped down on his chair at the breakfast table. "When did you and Mom get home from the hospital?"

"We came home just after midnight, Tim," Dad answered. "I've got some bad news for you. That pneumonia was just too much for your Grandpa. He died shortly before we left."

Tim sat quietly for a few minutes, thinking about Grandpa.

"I guess Grandpa would call that good news, Dad," said Tim. "He had been waiting for that to happen for a long time."

"Good news, Tim? What do you mean?"

"You know, Dad, Grandpa told me about dying one afternoon when I was visiting with him. He said he was a lot like his old friend Simeon when it came to dying."

"I don't recall Grandpa having a friend named Simeon," said Dad.

"This Simeon lived in Bible times," said Tim. "He must have been really old—older even than Grandpa. Grandpa said one day when Simeon was in church in Jerusalem, Mary and Joseph came in. They were carrying their new baby, Jesus, and two pigeons. Grandpa said it was the law that they had to bring the baby 40 days after He was born to present Him to God, and the pigeons were some sort of sacrifice."

Dad smiled. "Now I know the Simeon you're talking about. Grandpa read about him in that Bible he always kept beside his bed. God had told Simeon he wouldn't die until he had seen the Christ. And when Mary and Joseph and Jesus came in, the Holy Spirit told him that this Baby was the one. Simeon must have been happy to see that."

"Oh, yes," said Tim. "Grandpa said that Simeon praised God. He told God that now he could die in peace because he had seen the salvation God had sent in that little Baby Jesus."

"Maybe that's what made your Grandpa so ready to die, too, Tim," said Dad.

"I'm sure it is, Dad. Grandpa may never have met Simeon personally, but he certainly had seen the one Simeon was talking about. Grandpa told me that he believed his good Friend, Jesus, had died for him. That's why he was ready to die in peace like Simeon. Today I know that he's with his Friend, Jesus—and Simeon too—in heaven."

Shining Like Stars

Bible Reference: Matt. 2:1–12.

Materials: A large paper star covered with foil

Where have you seen stars? *Show the star and encourage the children to suggest answers.* You might see stars many places—in the sky, of course, or on a police officer's badge, or maybe on the dressing room door of a singer or actor. But after Christmas we think about a special star that God used to show people the way to His Son.

Soon after Jesus was born in Bethlehem, Wise Men from the east came looking for Him. These Wise Men were astrologers—men who studied the stars. They had seen a bright new star and knew it meant that the King of the Jews had been born. They followed that star all the way to Jerusalem. There they went to the palace, the place where they figured the new King must be.

But when they asked about the newborn King, no one knew what they meant. When King Herod heard about it, he began to worry. He didn't want anyone else to take his place as king. So he asked some teachers who studied the Bible, "Where will the Christ be born?"

"The prophet wrote that He will be born in Bethlehem in Judea," they answered.

So King Herod called for the Wise Men. He asked them some questions about the star they had followed. Then he told them, "You'll find the King in Bethlehem. And when you find Him, come back and report to me, so I may go worship Him too."

King Herod had lied to the Wise Men. He had no intention of worshiping Jesus.

The star led the Wise Men to Bethlehem. It rested right over the house where Mary, Joseph, and Jesus lived. The Wise Men had found the King they were looking for. They bowed down and worshiped Him. They gave Him the precious gifts they had brought with them.

God used the star to show the Wise Men the way to Jesus. When they found Him, they worshiped Him and gave Him gifts.

God can use you the same way He used that star. He can use you to lead people to Jesus. You can shine like that star by telling someone in your family how much you love Jesus. You can invite that person to go with you to church and Sunday school next week, or to pray with you before you go to bed.

You shine when you forgive a classmate who has hurt you, because you know that Jesus has forgiven you for the wrong things you have done. The love that you show reflects Jesus' love for your classmate and leads her to her Savior too.

God may lead you to shine like that star by becoming a pastor, missionary, or teacher when you grow up. Or you may shine as a Sunday school teacher or a singer in the choir. You might shine as a doctor or an engineer or a mechanic and tell your neighbors and the people you work with about your Savior, Jesus.

Ask Jesus to use you as one of His stars to lead people to Him. And then start looking for places to shine!

What Can I Give the Baby?

Bible Reference: Matt. 2:1–12.

Materials: A box wrapped as a baby gift, 10 $1 bills.

Have you ever shopped for a gift for a new baby? If you have, you probably remember going to the store and looking at all the pretty baby clothes and blankets. Perhaps you even checked out the car seats and highchairs and strollers. Maybe you decided to buy a stuffed animal or toy for the baby instead. After you decided on the perfect gift, you paid for it, brought it home, and wrapped it in pretty baby paper, like this. *Show baby gift.* Your gift was all ready to give to the baby.

Why did you spend so much time and money on the right gift for the new baby? *Allow children to respond.* Your gift shows how you feel about the baby. It shows that you love the baby and are happy about its birth.

But what if you went to the store with $10 for a baby gift and decided that you really didn't have to spend all of your money. *Hold up the 10 $1 bills.* Suppose you found a tiny rattle that cost $1. *Remove $1 from the rest.* That would leave you $9 for yourself. *Put $9 back in your pocket.* Or what if you decided to give your old, ragged bear to the new baby and keep all of the money for yourself?

What would this show about the way you feel about the baby? By keeping most of the gift money for yourself, you would show that you didn't really care much about the baby. You would show that you cared much more about yourself.

Soon after God's Son, Jesus, was born, Wise Men from the east came to worship Him. Like all visitors who come to see a new baby, they brought Jesus gifts. Their gifts—gold, frankincense, and myrrh—were very, *very* expensive. These gifts showed their love for Jesus. They also showed that the Wise Men knew that Jesus was a very special Baby, the one who was born King of the Jews.

Like the Wise Men, we bring gifts to Jesus when we come to worship Him. And our gifts, like theirs, show what we really think of Him. We can give just a little, keeping everything else for ourselves, or we can give generously, showing that we love Him and recognize that He is the Savior God sent for us.

We can give Him one hour for Sunday school once in a while, or we can give Him our time every day, time for worship and Bible study and family devotions. We can help our best friend who we know will pay us back, or we can look for ways to do kind things for all who need our help, even those who cannot help us in return. We can keep the good news about God's Son to ourselves, or we can tell our friends and neighbors what Jesus, our Savior, means to us and invite them to come learn more about Him. We can give a little, or we can give ourselves.

How will you decide what to give Jesus? God's Holy Spirit will help you remember Jesus' great love for you. We love Him because He loved us so much He gave His life for us.

 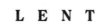

Bad Advice from a Snake

Bible Reference: Gen. 3:1–24.

Materials: A newspaper with an advice column.

Have you ever read a column like this in the newspaper? *Show column and read a sample letter.* This column has letters from people who are looking for advice. The person who writes the column answers the letters and tells the person what she thinks he or she ought to do.

For example, a man might ask the columnist how to get his brother to pay back the money he owes him. Or a woman may want advice on how to make friends in a new neighborhood. Boys and girls might ask for advice about whether to use cigarettes or drugs or alcohol.

Often the columnist's advice is good and helps the person solve the problem. But sometimes, because the columnist doesn't know the person well, the advice is bad. Following bad advice can bring more trouble than the person had in the first place.

When God first made the world, He put Adam and Eve into a beautiful, perfect garden. God provided everything that Adam and Eve needed. He told them they could eat fruit from any tree except the tree in the middle of the garden. They were never cold or hungry, never sad or sick, and they never sinned. God was their Friend and visited them often.

But one day Eve met another visitor in the garden. The devil had hidden himself in a snake. The snake said, "Did God really tell you not to eat from any tree in the garden?"

"We may eat fruit from all the trees," answered Eve. "But God did say not to eat from the tree in the middle of the garden or even touch it, or we'll die."

"Oh, you won't really die," advised the snake. "That fruit will make you like God. You will know good and evil."

Eve liked the snake's advice. After all, she thought, why should God always be the one in charge? Why shouldn't Adam and I be wise like He is? So Eve ate some of the fruit, and she gave some to her husband, Adam.

As soon as they had eaten the fruit, Adam and Eve knew they had sinned. When they heard God walking in the garden, they felt ashamed and hid in the bushes.

But God already knew Adam and Eve had disobeyed Him. Although their sin made Him very angry, God still loved Adam and Eve.

God punished Adam and Eve for their sin. He sent them out of the beautiful garden. He told them they would have to work hard to stay alive. They would experience sickness and sadness, and sin would fill their lives. And finally they would die.

But God also promised to send His own Son to be the answer to the problem of sin. God's Son would suffer and die, but He would end sin's control over people. By His death He would take the punishment that Adam and Eve deserved. Because of His death Adam and Eve—and all who believe in Him—will live with Him forever in heaven.

Saved by a Boat

Bible Reference: Gen. 6:1–9:17.

Materials: A toy boat.

If you have ever visited the ocean or one of the Great Lakes, you may have seen boats belonging to the United States Coast Guard. The men and women of the Coast Guard conduct search and rescue missions. They help people who are in trouble on the water—fishermen, pleasure boaters, or the passengers and crews of commercial boats. *Show the children your boat.* If a boat loses power or is involved in an accident, the Coast Guard rushes to the scene to rescue the people. Without the help of the Coast Guard, many people would die.

Long ago God conducted a special rescue by boat. After Adam and Eve left the Garden of Eden, they had many children. Their children also produced children, until the world was full of people. Most of these people did not love God and did not obey Him at all. Only one family loved and obeyed God—the family of Noah.

God planned to punish all of the wicked people by sending a huge flood to drown them. But He planned to rescue Noah and his family, who believed in Him.

God told Noah to build a boat—an ark. He told him exactly how big to make it and what kind of materials to use. When the ark was finished, God told Noah to put every kind of animal into it. He told him to store food for the animals and for his family. When Noah and his family and all of the animals were on board, God shut the door of the ark.

Then God did exactly as He had said. He sent rain for 40 days and nights. The water rose higher and higher until even the highest mountains were covered. All of the wicked people died. But Noah and his family floated safely in the ark.

Finally the rain stopped and the water started to go away. After many weeks the boat came to rest on top of a mountain. Noah, his family, and the animals stepped out on dry ground.

Noah built an altar beside the ark. He and his family thanked and praised God for saving them from the flood. God told Noah that He would never destroy the world with a flood again. He put a rainbow in the sky to remind Noah of His promise.

When we see a rainbow, we remember how God saved Noah and his family with a boat. We also think about the way He saves us.

God still hates sin. Although He doesn't send great floods to punish sinners today, His Word tells us that the punishment for sin is still death. And we are sinners.

But God has rescued all who love Him and believe in Him. He sent His Son, Jesus, to take the punishment in our place. Because Jesus died for our sins, we have been saved—just like Noah—from the punishment God sends. Like Noah, we thank and praise the one who rescued us—God's Son, Jesus.

His One and Only Son

Bible Reference: Genesis 22.

Materials: A wrapped candy bar.

Do you have a favorite kind of candy bar? *Show candy.* This is my very favorite. Normally I would only be able to show you an empty wrapper, because I usually eat the candy bar as soon as I get out of the store. But there's a good reason I haven't eaten this one.

I've given up eating candy bars for Lent. I didn't have to give them up. But I decided to give up something I love to remind myself of what God gave up for me.

Long ago, before Jesus was born, a man named Abraham believed in God and obeyed Him. God was so pleased with Abraham's faith that He called Abraham His friend.

God promised to give Abraham many descendants. He promised to make them a great nation. He even promised that the Savior would be one of Abraham's descendants. But Abraham had no children.

When Abraham and his wife, Sarah, were very old, God answered their prayers and sent them a son, as He had promised. Abraham nearly burst with happiness as he watched young Isaac grow up. He knew that, through Isaac, God would keep His promise to give Abraham more descendants than the stars in the sky. Abraham loved Isaac very much.

One day God told Abraham, "Take your son, Isaac, up to Mount Moriah. I want you to sacrifice him to Me there."

Abraham could hardly believe his ears. But the next morning he and Isaac and two servants began the long walk to Mount Moriah. Near the mountain, Abraham and Isaac left the servants to wait and walked on alone. Isaac carried the wood for the sacrifice, and Abraham carried the fire and the knife.

"Father," asked Isaac, "we have fire and wood, but where is the lamb for the sacrifice?"

"God will provide the lamb for the sacrifice," answered Abraham. And the father and son walked on.

When they reached the place God showed them, Abraham built an altar and prepared to kill his only son. But God called to Abraham from heaven. "Stop! Don't hurt the boy," God said. "Now I know how much you love Me, since you were willing to give Me your only son."

Because of his faith in God, Abraham was willing to give up Isaac, the son he loved so much. God understood that kind of love—He also gave up His only Son, Jesus. He sent Jesus to earth as a human being, then allowed Him to suffer and die in our place, to take the punishment we deserved for our sins.

My love for candy bars is nothing compared to Abraham's love for Isaac or God's love for Jesus and for us. But giving up candy bars for Lent reminds me every day of what God gave up to save me and make me His child.

Welcome Home

Bible Reference: Luke 15:11–32.

Materials: A length of yellow ribbon.

Have you ever seen a yellow ribbon tied around the trunk of a tree? Did you wonder what that ribbon was doing there?

A few years ago a popular song told the story of the yellow ribbons. The man in the story had done some terrible things. He had been convicted and sentenced to spend three years in jail. He had not seen or heard from his family in all the time he was in jail.

In jail the man had plenty of time to think about his family. "The things I did have made life very difficult for my wife and children," he thought. "People at home hate them because of what I did. While I am here in jail, they have had to work hard to survive. They must be ashamed to even know me."

When the man's jail term was almost over, he wrote a letter to his family. "I will be coming home on the bus next Friday," he wrote. "If you never want to see me again, I will understand. That's what I deserve. I'll just stay on the bus and go somewhere else. But if you want me to come back, tie a yellow ribbon around the old oak tree in the front yard."

As the man rode the bus toward home, he wondered what he would see. He told his story to the other passengers, and they helped him watch and wait.

When the bus finally rounded the curve before the man's house, a loud cheer rose from all the passengers on the bus. Hundreds of yellow ribbons covered the oak tree in front of the little house. The man was welcomed home.

Jesus wanted people to understand that His Father forgives and welcomes sinners. So He told a story about a boy who asked his father to give him his share of the money he would receive when his father died. The boy took the money to another country and wasted all of it. When the boy had nothing to eat and no one to help him, he thought about his father. "I'm going back to my father's house, where there is plenty of food," he said. "I'll tell him I'm sorry and ask if I can work for him as his servant. After what I did, I don't deserve to be his son."

When the father saw his son coming, he ran to him and hugged him tightly. "Father, I'm sorry," said the boy. "I don't deserve to be your son."

But the father called to his servants and said, "Bring the best clothes and put them on my son! Put a ring on his finger and shoes on his feet! Fix a big feast for all our friends! For my son who was lost has been found!"

We have sinned against our heavenly Father, and we don't deserve to be His children. But He gave His only Son, Jesus, to die for us. Because of Jesus our Father welcomes us back into His family and will welcome us into our heavenly home.

God's Ending

Bible Reference: Luke 19:28–40.

Materials: Optional: two palm leaves, one folded into a cross, or similar objects cut from paper. See the directions in the Appendix.

On Palm Sunday, everyone who came to my church received a leaf of a palm branch to carry into worship. The palms reminded us of the branches the children waved to welcome Jesus to Jerusalem on the first day of Holy Week.

As I left the church after the service, I noticed Aunt Adah still sitting in her pew, working hard on something. She was lovingly weaving the palm leaves into little crosses. *If you are using palm leaves, demonstrate how to make a cross.*

If I had written the story of Jesus, I would have ended it on Palm Sunday. It would be the story of a poor boy, born in a stable and cradled in a manger, who grew up in a carpenter's shop in Galilee. He became a traveling preacher, and in His three-year career He attracted ever-increasing crowds of people who were amazed to see Him heal people who were sick or crippled or blind or deaf. They ate the bread and fish He miraculously supplied and listened to His everyday stories about His Father's kingdom. They stared in wonder as He called His dead friend, Lazarus, from his grave. Sure, He had a few run-ins with the authorities, but in religion and politics that can happen. He Himself had said that a prophet is without honor in his own country. Finally He rode triumphantly into the capital city, hailed by a groundswell uprising of people whose coats became His red carpet, who waved palm branches and sang His praises as the successor to King David himself.

People like that kind of story. I would have ended it there, without the blood and the tears, the death and despair. Without the sacrifice.

But Palm Sunday was the first day of the week. Still to come were the supper and the garden, the betrayal and the trials, the scourging and mocking, and the agonizing death on Friday. Finally Jesus Himself cried out, "It is finished." The work God had sent Him to do, the punishment He took in our place, was done. All that was left was a borrowed tomb and the Sabbath rest of Saturday.

But the inspired Gospel writers go on. On the first day of the week women took the spices they had prepared to anoint a body that wasn't there. "Why do you look for the living among the dead? He is not here; He has risen!" the angels told them. This isn't an end—it's a beginning! A beginning of a new life for us: A glorious life with God, free from the separation from God caused by sin. And this life has no end.

God had lovingly woven the palm branches into a cross and from the end made a beginning for you and me.

Aren't you glad I didn't write the ending for the story? Aren't you glad God did?

A Bad Day That Was Good

Bible Reference: Luke 23:33–49.

Materials: A paper plate.

Before you begin: Draw a happy/sad face on the paper plate as shown in the Appendix.

Have you ever drawn a face like this to show that something made you happy? *Show the plate; then reverse the plate to show a sad face.* What does a face that looks like this mean?

Suppose your grandparents took you to the zoo. They let you spend as much time as you wanted watching your favorite animals, and they bought you ice cream and peanuts before you even asked. Which face would tell about your day? *Allow the children to turn the face in the right direction.* What if you woke up on the day of the school picnic and found it was raining? Which face would show how you felt?

Once in a while a day can be sad and happy at the same time. My friend Kerry had a day like that. Her father had a new job in a different town. Kerry was sad to leave her friends and her school and her church. *Turn to sad face.* But Kerry had visited the town where her family was going to move. She was excited about her pretty room in the new house and the swimming pool in the park just down the street. *Turn to happy face.*

A day can be sad and happy at the same time. In fact, the very worst day that ever happened is called good.

After Jesus grew up, He spent three years traveling from town to town, feeding the hungry, healing the sick and blind and crippled, and teaching people about God. Many people believed what Jesus said. They were happy that He had come to bring God's kingdom.

But some of the leaders did not like Jesus. They were jealous when people came to listen to Him and see the miracles He did. They worried that soon everyone would follow Jesus instead of them. So they planned to kill Jesus.

Jesus knew what the leaders were planning. He knew that it would hurt to die. But He also knew that dying was the only way He could save people from their sins.

Late one Thursday night, Jesus' enemies came to a garden where He was praying. They took Him away to be tried. At His trials, soldiers beat Him and pushed a crown of thorns on His head. Others told lies about Him and made fun of Him. All of His friends ran away.

Early Friday morning the governor said Jesus must die on a cross. More soldiers led Him to the edge of Jerusalem, where they nailed His hands and feet to the cross. He hung on the cross until He finally died.

What a terrible day this was for Jesus! Even the sky turned dark as night in the middle of the day, and the earth shook.

Just before Jesus died, He shouted, "It is finished." Finished for Him. Finished for us. By His death Jesus finished the work He had to do to rescue us—finished the sadness of our long separation from God.

A bad day for Jesus but a very Good Friday for us

When Empty Is Better

Bible Reference: Luke 24:1–12.

Materials: Two gift-wrapped empty boxes.

Do you like to get presents? I certainly do. As soon as I see a box wrapped like this, I can't wait to open it and see what's inside. I wonder if it could be something to wear, a book or a new game to play, or maybe even something to eat. I can hardly think about anything else until I get to open that present and find out what's inside for me.

Suppose someone gave you a present like this. *Show the children the first empty package.* Are you anxious to see what's in the box? Let's open it now. *Give the package to one of the children to open.*

What did you get? *Let the child show that the box is empty.* Were you disappointed when you saw that the box was empty?

We would all be upset if we opened a present and discovered the box was empty. That's because we really expected to find something nice inside. But what if you expected the box to contain something bad?

Suppose I tell you this box is full of poisonous spiders. Are you anxious to open the box now? Let's open it and see what's inside. *Give the second box to a child to open.*

How did you feel when you saw the box was empty? I know I felt really relieved. An empty box is much better than a box full of something awful.

I once read a story in the newspaper about a car that drove off the road and into the river. A passing motorist noticed the car's lights in the water and called the police. Police officers used the car's license number to find the name of the owner. They called the woman who owned the car to come down to the river while they pulled the car from the water.

The woman stood on the river bank in terror. Her son had borrowed her car that night to drive to work. She knew that when the car was pulled from the water, it would probably hold the body of her son.

Finally the car stood on the river bank. When the officers opened the door, only water ran out. The son's body was not in the car. Later the young man was found alive on the opposite shore of the river. He had been able to free himself from the car when it went into the river. The ecstatic mother thanked God that the car was empty.

On the Sunday morning after Jesus died on the cross, some women brought spices to His tomb. They expected to find Jesus' body in the tomb. But the tomb was empty. Jesus had risen! The women ran back to the city to tell Jesus' friends the good news that the tomb was empty.

Jesus' empty tomb is good news for us too. He died and rose for us. Because His grave was empty, we know that ours will be empty too—that even though we will someday die on earth, we will live with Him in heaven forever.

Because He Lives

Bible Reference: 1 Cor. 15:20, 42–44.

Materials: Several tulip bulbs.

I know a boy named Dave. Last summer Dave's dad became very sick. Doctors sent him to a big hospital in the city. There they discovered that he had cancer. The doctors operated to remove his tumors. They ordered several kinds of painful treatments. Yet, just before school started, Dave's dad died.

Because Dave is my friend, I went to the funeral. The pastor told how Dave's dad trusted in Jesus even though he was very, very sick. The pastor said that Jesus is the Resurrection and the Life. He told us that people who believe in Jesus, even though they die, will live with Him forever.

After the service we went to the cemetery. The pastor read some Bible verses and said some prayers. Then the casket with Dave's father's body was lowered into the ground.

I looked at Dave and his mother. They were crying. I felt so sorry for them that I cried too.

A few weeks later I stopped at a garden shop and bought some tulip bulbs to plant in front of my house. As I dug the holes for the bulbs, I thought about the cemetery and Dave's dad.

These bulbs are really pretty ugly, I thought—brown and misshapen and dirty—a lot like us, in a way, when sin distorts our lives, and sickness and trouble scar and soil us. These bulbs don't look like anything beautiful could come from them, and neither do we. And now I was burying the bulbs in holes in the earth, just as Dave's dad had been buried.

But even as I buried the bulbs, I knew what would happen. In spring, tulip plants, alive with colorful flowers, would grow where I had planted the bulbs. I knew because I had planted tulip bulbs before. I had already seen what happens.

I know that Dave's dad will live again, too—not in a sick, sinful body but in a glorious new body God will give him in heaven. I'm sure of that for the same reason I'm sure the tulips will grow and bloom. I've seen it happen before—to Jesus.

Jesus lived. Jesus died. He was buried, like the tulip bulbs and Dave's dad. And Jesus came alive again.

Jesus said, "I am the Resurrection and the Life. He who believes in Me will live, even though he dies; and whoever lives and believes in Me will never die" *(John 11:25)*. He promised, "Because I live, you also will live" *(John 14:19)*.

In spring, when I see the pretty tulips, I think of Dave's dad. I think of Jesus. And I think of the life in heaven that Jesus will give to all of us who believe in Him.

Forgiven to Feed Sheep

Bible Reference: John 21:15–19.

Materials: A magnifying glass, a cross sticker.

Did you ever feel that someone could see what you're thinking? Sometimes this happens when we have done something wrong. We feel as if our parents or teachers can look right into our heads with magic magnifying glasses. *Look at the children through the magnifying glass.* We are afraid that they know what we have done

Jesus' disciple, Peter, had good reason to feel guilty. On the night before He died, Jesus had told His friends that they would all desert Him. "Not me!" blustered Peter. "I'm ready to go with You to prison and to death."

"Peter," said Jesus, "before the rooster crows today, you'll deny three times that you even know Me."

Peter didn't think this was possible. But later that night, a frightened Peter warmed himself by the fire in the courtyard of the high priest. A servant girl asked if he had been with Jesus. "Woman, I don't even know Him," Peter responded.

A little later someone else pointed at Peter and said, "You're also one of them."

Now Peter was really scared. "Man, I am not!" he exploded.

Still another man recognized Peter. "You're from Galilee, like Jesus."

Peter panicked. "I don't know what you're talking about," he lied. Just as he said this, the rooster crowed, and Peter remembered what Jesus had said.

After saying he didn't know Him, Peter wondered if Jesus still loved him. Even though he was very sorry, he didn't know if Jesus would still want to be his friend. Then one day Jesus met His disciples on a beach in Galilee. After a breakfast of fish, Jesus spoke to Peter.

"Simon, son of John," He said, "do you truly love Me more than these?"

Maybe Peter squirmed and felt like we do when we think people can see our thoughts. *Hold up magnifying glass.* "Yes, Lord," he answered, "You know that I love You."

Jesus said, "Feed My lambs." Then Jesus asked Peter again, "Do you really love Me?"

Peter answered, "You know that I love You."

Jesus replied, "Take care of My sheep." Then Jesus asked the third time, "Do you love Me?"

"Lord," Peter said, "You know all things; You know that I love You."

Jesus said, "Feed My sheep." Jesus told Peter that he was going to spend his life telling others about Jesus and would finally be killed for being Jesus' disciple.

Now Peter knew that Jesus had seen what was going on inside his head. *Put cross sticker on magnifying glass.* But he knew that Jesus saw it with the forgiveness He had won for Peter on the cross. Jesus still loved Peter and wanted him to be His friend and disciple.

Look at the children through the magnifying glass with the cross sticker. God looks at us through the cross too. He forgives us and calls us friends because of Jesus.

What Makes a Good Shepherd Good?

Bible Reference: John 10:11–15.

Materials: Picture of a boy and dog (see Appendix).

Jimmy had taken care of Buster ever since Buster was a puppy. Every morning he filled Buster's dish with dry dog food. Every evening he gave him a can of dog food. Several times a day Jimmy put out fresh water for Buster to drink. He brushed Buster's shiny coat whenever it needed it, and he took Buster for a walk as soon as he got home from school.

"You're my dog, Buster," said Jimmy, "and I'll always love you." *Show picture.*

One summer Jimmy's family took a trip. Jimmy's mother asked Mary Lou to take care of Buster while they were gone. "We'll be gone for three days," said Mother. "Be sure to feed and water him every day. Brush him when he needs it, and take him for a walk. We'll pay you $2 for each day we're gone for taking care of Buster."

The first day Mary Lou fed and watered Buster in the morning and at night. She took him for a walk. "Hey, dog," she said to Buster, "I'll be back again tomorrow."

The second morning Mary Lou fed and watered Buster. But after supper she went to Nancy's house and forgot about feeding Buster.

On the third morning Mary Lou overslept. She finally went to feed Buster at noon. "Sorry, dog," she said. "Better late than never." Buster lay in his doghouse. His coat needed brushing. He wished someone would take him for a walk.

That evening Jimmy's family came home. Jimmy ran out to the doghouse. "Buster, Buster," he called. "I missed you. Did you miss me too?"

Buster was glad to hear Jimmy call his name. He wagged his tail and licked Jimmy's face. He knew Jimmy loved him and took care of him best because he was Jimmy's own dog.

Jesus said, "I am the good shepherd. The good shepherd lays down His life for the sheep. The hired hand is not the shepherd who owns the sheep. So when he sees the wolf coming, he abandons the sheep and runs away. The wolf attacks the flock and scatters it. The man runs away because he is a hired hand and cares nothing for the sheep. I am the good shepherd; I know My sheep and My sheep know Me."

Jesus, the Good Shepherd, knows everything we need. He cares for us and provides for us. Like sheep who wander away from the shepherd, we stray from Jesus when we sin. But Jesus, our Good Shepherd, looks for us until He finds us and carries us back home with Him.

We know Jesus is the best Shepherd of all. He proved it when He gave His life for us on the cross.

Sing to the Lord

Bible Reference: Ps. 96:1–4.

Wherever you visit a Christian church, you hear singing. It may be in a language you don't understand. The rhythms and melodies may sound strange to you. It might be accompanied by drums and cymbals. It could even be spelled out in sign language. But everywhere you go, you'll hear and see people using music to praise God.

That reminds me of Karen and her little sister. Karen had always wanted a little sister. She had been able to think of nothing else since her parents told her they were going to adopt a little girl from a Christian orphanage in China. After months of waiting the day came when Kim Li would arrive in the United States.

Early that morning Karen and her mother flew to Seattle, where they waited impatiently for Kim Li's plane to arrive from Taiwan. Finally the big jet landed, and a woman from the Chinese orphanage handed a beautiful black-haired two-year-old to Karen's mother. It was the happiest moment of Karen's life.

But by afternoon Karen began to wonder if her family had made a big mistake. Kim Li refused to eat any of her lunch in the airport restaurant. She couldn't understand anything Karen said to her. She cried and whined as they waited in the boarding lounge for the plane that would take them home. Mother said that Kim Li was tired from her long flight and frightened by the strange people and surroundings, but Karen began to worry that her sister would never be happy in her new family.

By the time the plane left Seattle, Kim Li's whining had turned to wailing. Other passengers stared angrily, and even the stewardess asked if there wasn't some way to quiet the little girl. Kim Li fought her way from Mother's lap to Karen's and screamed.

"Try singing to her," suggested Mother. "Maybe that will calm her down."

"Singing?" thought Karen. "I don't see how it will help, but I'm ready to try anything."

Karen began to sing softly. "Jesus loves me, this I know." Kim Li's crying grew softer as she listened to Karen's voice. "For the Bible tells me so." Kim Li stared into Karen's face. Now the only sound was Karen's voice. "Little ones to Him belong." A tiny smile curled Kim Li's mouth. "They are weak but He is strong," Karen finished the verse.

As Karen started the song's refrain, she heard a new sound—soft and clear and a little off-key: "Ju Yesu nai wo, Ju Yesu nai wo, Ju Yesu nai wo, Shung jing i ko ru wo." Kim Li's face brightened as she sang along with her new sister. Her tense little body relaxed, and soon she was fast asleep on Karen's lap.

Christians sing for many reasons: to praise God, to show how happy they are that He has saved them, to pray for His help, to tell others what He has done, and sometimes just to share their faith with each other as members of His family here on earth.

Up, Up, but Not Away

Bible References: Luke 24:50–53, Acts 1:1–14.

Materials: Picture of a child with Jesus (see Appendix).

Have you ever played peekaboo with a baby? If you put something—a large book or the baby's blanket—in front of your face, the baby thinks that you are gone. As soon as you remove the book or blanket, she laughs with delight to see you have returned.

Often a baby cries unhappily when her mother leaves the room. She hasn't developed the concept that Mother is still nearby, even though she can't see her.

Only babies consider peekaboo a thrilling game. Older children and adults know that someone may be close by even though they cannot see him. The baby will understand this concept as she grows older.

Jesus' disciples were confused like small children sometimes. After Jesus rose from the dead, He appeared to them on many occasions—in a room in Jerusalem, on the road to Emmaus, on a beach in Galilee. But He disappeared as suddenly as He had come. When Jesus wasn't with them, the disciples didn't know what to do.

Jesus was preparing them for the time when they would not be able to see that He was with them. He told them to stay in Jerusalem and wait for the gift He had promised. He said He would send His Holy Spirit to teach them all things and give them the power to work for Him.

One day Jesus took the disciples to the Mount of Olives. There He raised His hands and blessed them. He told them to tell everyone about Him in Jerusalem, Judea, Samaria, and to the ends of the earth. He promised that He would always be with them. Then, as the disciples watched, Jesus was taken up into heaven.

The disciples watched Jesus ascend until a cloud hid Him from their view. Then they noticed two angels standing with them. "Why are you staring up at the sky?" the angels asked. "Jesus has gone to heaven, but He will come back the same way you saw Him go."

The happy disciples walked back to Jerusalem to wait for the Spirit Jesus had promised to send. They knew that they would never be without Jesus. With the Holy Spirit's help, they would tell people all over the world about Him.

We love Jesus and are glad He is with us all the time. *Show picture of child with Jesus.* We know that He loves us and takes care of us. He protects us from the devil, who tries to make us sin. And He forgives us for the wrong things we do.

We can't see Jesus with us. *Cover the portion of the picture that shows Jesus.* But we still know He is there, just as He promised He would be. We can read about Him in His Word. We can talk to Him whenever we want to in prayer. He still loves us, protects us, and forgives us. And He still helps us when the devil wants us to sin. He touches us in a special way in Baptism and the Lord's Supper.

With the Holy Spirit, whom Jesus sent, we can tell others all the wonderful things our Savior has done for us, and we can know that He will always be with us.

Have You Seen the Holy Spirit?

Bible Reference: Acts 2:14–21.

Materials: One red balloon.

Before Jesus went back to heaven, He promised His disciples He would send them the Holy Spirit. The Holy Spirit would help them understand what Jesus had been saying and doing while He was with them. He would give them faith to trust in Jesus as their Savior. The Spirit would give them the power to tell others about Jesus, just as He had told them to do.

Fifty days after Easter, the disciples met together in a room in Jerusalem. Suddenly they heard a noise that sounded like a tremendous wind. They saw flames of fire on each other's heads. The Holy Spirit had come, just as Jesus promised.

The Holy Spirit filled each one of the disciples. They wanted to tell everyone about Jesus and how He had died to save them. They could even speak in languages they had never spoken before.

People from many countries were in Jerusalem that week to celebrate the Feast of Pentecost. When they heard the loud wind, they came to see what was going on. They were surprised to hear the disciples speaking in their own languages. They stayed to listen to what Peter and the others had to say.

Peter said, "Let me explain what happened. God has filled us with His Holy Spirit, just as the prophet Joel foretold. Now listen to this: God sent Jesus, whom you know, to live among you. It was God's plan that you would have Him nailed to the cross to die. But God raised Jesus from the dead."

I wish we had been there to hear the mighty wind and see the flames of fire. I wish we could have heard Peter preach to the people. It's hard to understand what the Holy Spirit is like when we can't see Him any more than we can see the air around us.

In a way, air is a little like the Holy Spirit. Although we can't see air, we can see the things it does. Trees bend in the wind. A sailboat races across a lake. A kite dances in the sky. And we continue to live because the air is around us for us to breathe.

We know the Holy Spirit is here because we see what He does. A little child receives faith in Jesus through Baptism. A young man reads the Bible and trusts Jesus as his Savior from sin. A shy woman tells her neighbor what a difference Jesus has made in her life and invites her to come along to church. The neighbor agrees to go and meets Jesus, her Savior.

You see, we don't really see air until it's inside something. *Begin to inflate the balloon.* We know the balloon has air in it because we see that it looks full. Because of the air inside, the balloon feels firm and strong. *Release the balloon.* And we know that the power that sends the balloon flying comes from the air inside.

We see the Holy Spirit when He is inside of Christians. We see Him in the fullness of their lives because they know Jesus. We see Him as they live out their firm, strong faith. We know their power comes from the Holy Spirit inside them.

A Picture of God

Bible Reference: Matt. 28:19.

Materials: Trinity pinwheel (see Appendix).

Wouldn't you like to know what God looks like? No one has ever seen God, because He is a spirit without a physical body. Even when God came to earth as a human being in the person of Jesus, nobody took His picture. The paintings of Jesus that we see are only artists' ideas of what He might have looked like.

I wanted to draw a picture of God. I tried to remember what the Bible said about Him. Then I made this picture. *Show children the Trinity pinwheel.* My picture doesn't look like a human being. It's not supposed to. But it does show what God is like.

My picture has three circles, just like God is three persons. Each of the circles is complete. But the circles do not stand alone. Linked together, the circles give us a picture of God.

Turn wheel so the hand is on top. The hand shows what God the Father does. He created the whole world from nothing. He takes care of everything He made: mountains and oceans, plants and animals, you and me. He provides everything we need to live. God the Father is really God. He is the first Person of the Holy Trinity.

Turn wheel so the cross is on top. When Adam and Eve spoiled God's perfect creation by disobeying Him, God promised to send them a Savior. Jesus, God's Son, came to earth as a human being. He obeyed God's law perfectly. Then He died on the cross, taking the punishment for our sin. Jesus rose from the dead and went back to His heavenly Father. But we know He will come back one day to judge the earth and to take everyone who believes in Him to heaven. Jesus, God's Son, is also really God. He is the second Person of the Holy Trinity.

Turn wheel so the heart is on top. The Holy Spirit fills our hearts with faith in Jesus, our Savior. Through God's Word, Baptism, and the Lord's Supper, He plants that faith and makes it grow. He gives us the power to be Christians and live the way God wants us to live. He helps us tell other people about Jesus. The Holy Spirit is really God. He is the third Person of the Holy Trinity.

Just as all three of the circles in my picture are the same size, so all three Persons—Father, Son, and Holy Spirit—are of the same importance. Each one is God. *Point to the center section of the wheel.* But there are not three Gods. Only One.

So we believe in one God, the Holy Trinity—one God who made and cares for us, who died to save us, and who puts faith in our hearts.

What Shape Is Love?

Bible Reference: 1 John 4:7–12.

Materials: The following shapes: heart, baby bottle, dog bone, teddy bear, car key, diamond ring, cross (see Appendix).

On Valentine's Day we like to send each other pretty cards shaped like this. *Show the heart.* What does this shape mean?

On Valentine's Day, or any other day, a heart always makes us think of love. We sometimes see cars with bumper stickers that say, "I ♥ my dog." Parents and children leave each other notes that read, "I ♥ U."

But the heart isn't the only shape that means love. In fact, different shapes mean love to different people.

A tiny baby doesn't know about valentine hearts. He only thinks of his hungry tummy and the warm milk he needs to fill it. To the tiny baby, this shape means love. *Show the baby bottle.* The baby comes to love the person who gives him his bottle.

Your pet can't read love notes. But it loves the person who feeds it, plays with it, and takes care of it. If your pet is a dog, this shape might mean love. *Show the bone.*

As children grow, they find special "friends" to love. These friends comfort them when they are sick or lonely, and they're always ready to play. To a small girl or boy, perhaps this shape means love. *Show the teddy bear.*

As children grow up, they need different things. One girl wished for a special present for her 16th birthday—something she could drive to school and to her part-time job. The little present her parents gave her rattled in its box and looked like this and fit in a big present that was parked outside. *Show the car key.* To the girl, this shape showed her parents' love.

Some years later this young woman fell in love with a wonderful young man. One day he asked her to marry him and be his wife. He gave her a gift that was shaped like this. *Show the diamond ring.* When the young woman looked at the gift, she saw her sweetheart's love.

What shape would you use to show God's love?

You might choose the sun or the moon, a mountain or tree, an animal or plant—any of the wonderful things He created. Or you might choose your favorite food or your house or a bottle of medicine to show one of the ways He takes care of you. You could pick the parents He gave you or your own marvelous body. All of these show His love for us.

But God chose to show His love with this shape. *Show the cross.* Even though we disobey Him, He sent His Son, Jesus, to take the punishment for our sin. When Jesus died on the cross, He showed us just how much God really loves us.

When you see this shape *show the heart*, think of the many different ways people show their love for you. And when you see this *show the cross*, remember the cross-shaped love of God.

Every Day Is Mother's Day

(And Father's Day, Son's Day, and Daughter's Day Too)

Bible Reference: Eph. 4:29–32.

Materials: Two handwritten notes, one in a child's writing and the other in an adult's, both reading: I'm sorry for the things I said. Please forgive me. Aren't you glad Jesus forgives us too? P.S. I love you. (See Appendix.) Fold each note several times.

It certainly wasn't Mother's Day when these notes were written!

Hillary had never been in a worse mood. As soon as she started to pull on her favorite jeans, she remembered she had never asked Mom to fix the broken zipper. She tossed the jeans back on the floor, slipped into the red jumper she hated, and stomped into the kitchen .

"Eat fast," said Mom without even looking at Hillary. "I have to drop you off at school, take Kyle to the sitter's, and still get to work in time for an 8 o'clock meeting."

"You sure worry a lot about your schedule," grumbled Hillary. "You'd think you could at least take the time to fix my jeans' zipper."

"Zipper? If you ever cleaned up your room, we might find things like that in time. Hurry! Is your backpack ready?"

Hillary reached for the math papers she had left on the floor last night. "Yikes!" she yelled. "Kyle scribbled all over my homework. Can't you control him at all?"

Mom picked up Kyle and shoved Hillary out the door. "I am sick and tired of all the complaints around here. If you don't like living here, young lady, you can just move out."

Hillary rode to school in silence. But when she got out of the car, she gave the door an extra hard slam. Kyle cried.

That night Hillary got ready for bed. After she crawled under the covers, she lay awake and thought for a long time. She thought of some things she must do before she went to sleep. After she did them, she went back to bed and fell sound asleep.

Hillary's mother sat in the chair in front of the TV, but she paid no attention to the program. She thought about Hillary. Finally she went to her desk. She took out a paper and pencil and wrote Hillary this note. *Unfold Mom's note and read it.* "I'm sorry for the things I said. Please forgive me. Aren't you glad Jesus forgives us too? P.S. I love you." She folded the note and took it to Hillary's bedroom.

The first thing Mom noticed was that Hillary had picked up all the clothes and toys from her floor and put them away. The second thing she noticed was a folded piece of paper on top of Hillary's covers. Mom unfolded the paper and read Hillary's note. *Unfold child's note.* "I'm sorry for the things I said. Please forgive me. Aren't you glad Jesus forgives us too? P.S. I love you."

Mom smiled. Forgiveness felt mighty good. "Thank You, God," she said, "for loving and forgiving us both. Amen."

Greater Love Hath No Man Than This

Bible Reference: John 15:9–17.

Materials: A geranium or other small flowering plant.

Show plant. On Memorial Day we often take flowers like this to the cemetery. We plant the flowers on the graves of friends or family members who have died. We don't do this because we think the person who is dead will enjoy the flowers. We bring flowers because bringing them helps us to remember our friend or relative.

When I was a child, I went with my mother on Memorial Day to plant flowers on my grandfather's grave. As I waited for my mother, I watched an old man with a cane carry a pot of flowers up the little hill to the grave next to Grandpa's. He wore a faded uniform, the kind soldiers wore long ago. Painfully he knelt on the ground next to the headstone and began to dig.

Mother was still planting, so I wandered over to read the headstone behind the man. The little flag next to the name told me that this person had been a soldier too.

I watched in silence until the man in the uniform had patted down the dirt around the plant on the grave. Then I asked politely, "Was this man a friend of yours?"

The old soldier looked up at me. He thought for a long time. "I guess you could say he was the best friend I ever had. We were together all through the war. In France we saw the very worst of the fighting. Then one day several of us were loading supplies into a jeep. We heard the hiss of a grenade heading right for us. We stared as it landed a few feet in front of us, too paralyzed by fear to even try to move away. But my friend … " the soldier paused. "My friend, without even thinking what to do, threw himself on the grenade, saving us from the force of its explosion."

He patted the dirt around the plant again. "My friend gave his life so I could live. There's no way I can repay him. That's why I'm here with these flowers—just to remember him and what he did for me."

As I watched the old soldier limp back down the hill, I felt jealous. I wished I had a friend who loved me the way his friend had loved him, enough to die for him. And then I remembered. I do.

And when I remember what my best Friend, Jesus, did for me, I know there's no way I can repay Him either. But I remember Him and what He did for me by loving and serving those around me, by living the way He wants me to live, by worshiping Him with the other friends He died to save. And I will make sure everyone knows what Jesus, my greatest Friend, has done for me.

Fathers: Models of God

Bible Reference: Luke 11:11–13.

Materials: A model car, the kind made from a kit.

Have you ever made a model car? *Show model to the children.*

Many children enjoy making and collecting models. They like following the directions and gluing the tiny pieces together. They enjoy positioning the decals and painting the trim. They feel proud when they can display their finished models.

You can learn a lot from making model cars. You can learn to read directions and follow them carefully. You learn how the different parts of the car fit together. And, if you make several models, you learn how each of the cars is different from the others.

But most model builders agree that two things are important when choosing a model kit to build. They want the car to be a model of the real car they like best. And they want the model to be as much like the real car as possible.

Perhaps that's why God gave us fathers. God calls Himself our heavenly Father. Jesus told us to call God Father when we pray to Him. He even gave us a prayer to say, beginning, "Our Father, who art in heaven …" And then He gave us earthly fathers so we would have an incomplete picture—a model—of what He is like.

Our earthly fathers are good models when they look to the heavenly Father for their example. Our heavenly Father provides everything we, His children, need. He takes care of us and protects us from danger. He always has time to listen when we talk to Him. He sets rules for us—we call them the commandments—and He expects us to obey Him. He disciplines us in love. He never stops loving us, even though we sin. He forgives us for the sake of His Son, Jesus.

Just like a model car, our earthly fathers are the best models when they imitate God very closely. But earthly fathers are human. No matter how hard they try, they cannot be perfect models of God. Sometimes they get tired and cranky; sometimes they are impatient with their children. Stress leads to angry explosions and tears.

Christian fathers feel bad when this happens. They tell God they are sorry. They tell their children they are sorry too. They know that our heavenly Father gave His Son, Jesus, to die on the cross to pay for the sins of fathers and mothers and children. They know that God's forgiveness can heal the hurt that sin causes in a family. They know that God's love makes it possible for fathers, mothers, and children to love each other.

Proclaim Liberty

Bible Reference: John 8:34–36.

Materials: A picture of the Liberty Bell.

Do you know the name of this bell? *Show picture.* That's right, this is the Liberty Bell in Philadelphia. It rang on July 4, 1776, when the Declaration of Independence was read to the people of Philadelphia. If the picture were larger, you could see that the words on the Liberty Bell come from the Bible, from Leviticus 25:10—"Proclaim liberty throughout all the land unto all the inhabitants thereof."

The word *liberty* always makes me think of Papa Schlutski and his family. Papa Schlutski owned a delicatessen in the town where I grew up. My mother sent me to Papa's store whenever she ran out of bread or milk or eggs. On Saturday mornings I went to the deli with my father to choose which delicious sausages we would eat for Sunday supper and the next week's lunches.

I loved to go to Papa's store because I knew I would always find him there. If I stopped in early on my way to school, I knew Papa and Mrs. Schlutski would already be busy stuffing the fragrant meat into casings in the back room of the shop. While I spent the morning studying at school, Papa swept and cleaned and ordered groceries. In the afternoon, Mrs. Schlutski went to her other job, cleaning at the hospital, while Papa waited on customers. And late at night I could always find Papa restocking shelves for the next day's work.

"You must hate working all day and all night," I told Papa one day. "You're just a slave here in this store."

Papa suddenly became very serious. "A slave?" he said. "No, no, it's just the opposite. I work because I'm free. In Poland I was a slave. I started working before it was daylight. My wife and I worked hard all day long and far into the night. In Poland we were slaves."

"But, Papa," I said, "that's exactly what you do here!"

"It looks the same," Papa explained, "but here we work because we're free. In Poland, no matter how hard we worked, the government owned the shop, and our work made no difference. We could not raise our children the way we wanted; we could not worship in our own church. But here we have worked and saved our earnings. We bought our own store, which we manage as we please. Our sons attended college and found good jobs. And we close the store on Sundays and go to church together."

Jesus said, "Everyone who sins is a slave to sin" (*John 8:34*). That includes all of us, because we know that we sin every day. No matter how hard we try to do what is right, we continue in sin's slavery. But Jesus took our place, setting us free from sin when He died on the cross. He said, "If the Son sets you free, you will be free indeed" (*John 8:36*).

Free for what? Just like Papa Schlutski, we're free to work because we're free from sin, death, and the devil. We help and serve others, proclaiming the liberty Jesus gives us to everyone around us.

Don't Forget Your Flashlight

Bible Reference: Ps. 119:105–12.

Materials: A flashlight.

School begins this week. For many of us, the beginning of school means lots of back-to-school shopping. Can you make a list of the things you need to have to go back to school? *Allow the children to suggest items for the list.* Yes, pencils, crayons, scissors, rulers, notebooks, sneakers, sweaters, and jackets are all things we need to go back to school.

Did you think of putting a flashlight on your list? You could use the flashlight to search for little things that get lost in the pile of stuff that accumulates in the bottom of your desk or locker after a few months of school. Or you could keep it in your classroom in case the power goes out during a thunderstorm.

My friend Jeff needed a flashlight for school. Jeff rode a school bus every day from his house out in the country to the school in town. To catch the bus he had to walk through the woods to the end of his lane. When school started in September, it was light enough for Jeff to see where the lane curved between the trees and went up and down the hill. But by the end of October, Jeff had to make his morning walk in the dark. He knew he could easily step off the lane and twist his ankle in the soft dirt. He might slip on acorns or trip over a fallen branch.

So every morning Jeff put on his jacket and his backpack and picked up his flashlight. With the flashlight he could walk down the hilly, curvy lane without problems.

The Bible tells us that God's Word is a lamp for our feet and a light for our path. As we begin a new year of school, we know that there will be problems ahead. We might hurt a friend by saying something mean, or lie or cheat to get ahead in class. We may disobey our parents and teachers or not do the work that has been assigned. Sin causes us to slip and trip at school and at home.

But God's Word shows us Jesus, who died in our place. God forgives our sins for Jesus' sake when we tell Him we are sorry. God gives us the power of His Holy Spirit to help us live the way He wants us to live, as He shows us in His Word.

As you go back to school, take those pencils and crayons and notebooks. And don't forget your "flashlight." Let God's Word be the lamp for your feet and light for your path this school year and always.

Don't Forget to Say Thank You

Bible Reference: Luke 17:11–19.

Material: A piece of thank-you stationery.

When I was a child, my favorite days of the whole year were Christmas and my birthday. I loved those days for the same reason you love Christmas and your birthday—presents! I waited for the day to come, trying to guess what would be in those packages. When the day arrived, I could hardly finish my breakfast before diving into the brightly wrapped boxes. Presents, presents, presents—and all for me!

When I was a child, my least favorite days of the whole year were the days following Christmas and my birthday. Every day began the same. "Have you written your thank-you notes yet?" my mother would ask. How I hated writing thank-you notes!

After several days had passed, my mother would appear with a little box. "I bought you some new stationery," she would say. *Show thank-you stationery.* "That will make writing the thank-you notes easier." But it never seemed to help.

One Christmas my mother was especially busy and forgot about the notes, and I was glad to forget them too.

Then, one day in January, my grandmother came to visit. "Did you like the Christmas present I sent you?" she asked me.

"Oh, yes, Grandma," I answered. "I was just crazy about it."

"May I see what you did with it?" Grandma asked.

My brain raced as I tried desperately to remember the gift. But it was useless; I simply could not remember.

"Grandma," I said, "I guess I didn't appreciate your gift enough to write you a letter, and now I've even forgotten what it was. I'm really sorry."

Grandma put her arm around my shoulders. "Part of appreciating a gift is remembering to thank the giver. Our thankfulness shows the value we place on the gift.

"Jesus once healed 10 men who had a terrible skin disease called leprosy," Grandmother continued. "Nine of the men ran off to show the priests that they were healed. Only one of the men came back to thank Jesus. To whom do you think the healing meant the most?"

I knew what she meant. "The one who thanked Jesus," I answered. "I really am sorry, Grandma."

Grandma smiled at me. "I know," she said. "I forgive you, and Jesus does too. Because He died for us, we know for sure that all of our sins are forgiven."

I thought about what she had said. "I'm thankful for that," I said.

Grandma said, "Me too."

Is God Fair?

Bible Reference: Ex. 20:1–6.

Materials: Monopoly or another board game.

Have you ever played a game like this? *Show game and allow responses.*

Playing a board game can be lots of fun. You can choose which piece you want to use, throw the dice, and move your piece around the board. Sometimes you get to draw a special card and do whatever the card says to do. Sometimes you win the game; sometimes you lose.

But what would happen if you bought a new game and found that it had no rules? My friend Casey and her brother Pete bought a game like that at their neighbor's garage sale. Casey wanted to play the game anyway. So she and Pete started to play.

Casey chose the car piece, and she threw the dice first. She moved seven spaces. Pete chose the piece that looked like a shoe. He threw two sixes and moved 12 spaces. "That's doubles," said Pete, "so I get another turn."

"That's not fair!" yelled Casey. "There's no rule about doubles." She grabbed the dice away from Pete.

Casey threw a five. Her car landed on the same square as Pete's shoe. "I'm kicking you out," laughed Casey. "You have to go to jail." She moved Pete's piece to the jail square.

"No fair! No fair!" screamed Pete. He shoved the game board off the table and onto the floor. "If you won't play fair, I won't play with you at all!"

Playing a game with no rules would be almost as hard as living in a world without rules. People would cheat and hurt one another, and everyone would end up fighting.

Long ago God gave people rules to live by. The rules would help people treat each other fairly and live in peace. The rules would help people show their love for God. We call God's rules the Ten Commandments.

When God first gave the commandments to Moses, He expected His people to obey them. He told them He would punish everyone who disobeyed Him and show love to all who obeyed Him.

Was God being fair? Of course He was. After all, it was His world and His commandments.

The people listened to God's commandments and promised to obey. But even though they tried to do what God said, they often disobeyed Him—just like we disobey, even though we know how God wants us to live.

Because God is fair, He must punish everyone who sins. But God is also merciful. Even though we sin, He loves us. To save us from the punishment we deserved, He sent His Son, Jesus, to earth. Jesus obeyed God's commandments perfectly. Then God punished Jesus in our place. Now when God looks at us, He sees what Jesus did for us. Is that fair? No. Thank God, it's not. That's God's mercy.

No Other Gods
You shall have no other gods.

Bible Reference: Ex. 32:1–14.

Materials: A small animal figurine.

Long ago God gave His people the Ten Commandments. The people promised they would do as God said. God's First Commandment told the people they should only worship the real God. This was the most important commandment of all. But when their leader, Moses, went up on Mount Sinai to talk to God, the people broke the First Commandment.

God's people had just come from the land of Egypt, where they had lived as slaves. They knew that the Egyptians prayed to many gods. Some of these gods were statues of animals or people, like this. *Show figurine.* Others were the sun and the moon. Since the Egyptians were rich and powerful, God's people thought that their gods must be powerful too.

Now God's people were camped far out in the desert. God had spoken to them from the mountain and given them His Law, and His voice made them shake in their sandals. So Moses climbed up the mountain to write down God's Law on stone tablets for the people. The people hoped he would return soon.

But Moses was gone for 40 days and nights. The people thought he would never come back. So they asked Aaron, Moses' brother, to make a new, powerful god to lead them.

Aaron took the people's gold earrings, melted them, and molded them into a golden calf. "Here is your god who brought you out of Egypt," shouted Aaron. All of the people sang and danced to praise their new god.

Just then Moses came back to the camp and saw what the people were doing. He threw the stone tablets with God's Law on them to the ground and broke them. He burned the golden calf in the fire, ground its ashes, scattered them on the water, and made the people drink it.

Then Moses went back to talk to God. "My people have sinned against you," Moses said. "Please forgive their sins. If you cannot forgive them, punish me in their place."

Later Moses brought two new stone tablets up the mountain. God wrote His Law for the people again.

Worshiping or praying to a statue of an animal or person sounds silly to us, so we think we obey the First Commandment. But this commandment means that we must love God more than anything or anyone else. We break this commandment when we let money or possessions or fun become more important than God. We disobey when we love someone else enough to do what that person wants instead of what God wants us to do. We break it most often by letting what we want determine our actions.

We ask God to forgive us for breaking the First Commandment. Like Moses, Jesus said to God, "Punish Me in their place." And God did. Because Jesus took our punishment when He died on the cross, God forgives us.

Use It Right or Not at All

You shall not misuse the name of the LORD your God.

Bible Reference: Ex. 20:7.

Materials: A child's jacket.

When I was a child, I desperately wanted a jacket just like this one. *Show the jacket and explain what was so special about it.* I begged and pleaded, but Mother simply explained that the jacket I wanted was much too expensive, and I would have to make do with the jacket I had worn the year before.

Finally my birthday arrived. I opened the packages that were the right shape for toys first, then the ones that looked like they might contain clothes. To my delight, the last box I opened contained my precious jacket. I put it on immediately and wore it the rest of the day.

The next morning I put on my new jacket. "Be careful with that jacket," Mother said. "It was awfully expensive. Take good care of it, or don't wear it at all." I promised to take care of the jacket and tried to wipe away the jelly I had already spilled on it while Mother wasn't looking.

At recess time I wore my new jacket out on the playground. Since the weather had warmed up, my friends weren't wearing their jackets. I slipped mine off, too, and let it fall to the ground.

After recess one of the older kids knocked on our classroom door. "We found this jacket on the playground," he said. "Does it belong to someone in this room?"

The jacket looked like mine, but it was covered with dirt. I claimed the filthy jacket and hung it in my locker.

After school I tossed my dirty jacket in a corner of the garage and played with my friends until suppertime. When Mother came home from work, she asked about my jacket. "I don't see your new jacket. Did you hang it in the closet when you came home?"

My guilty look told her that I had not. Sheepishly I went out to the garage and brought her the jacket. "I'm really sorry, Mother," I said. "Is my jacket ruined?"

Mother looked at the dirty jacket. "You didn't take very good care of this jacket," she said. "I can see how bad you feel. Let's see if we can get it clean."

Then Mother loaded my jacket into the washing machine along with some strong soap. Before bedtime the jacket looked as good as new. "Now take care of the jacket," Mother said. "When you have something that is worth a lot, you must either use it right or not use it at all."

You could say the same thing about God's name. His name is very important and powerful. When we use His name to praise Him, to pray to Him, or to tell others about Him, we use it the right way. But when we use it any other way—for example, for swearing— we show that it isn't worth very much to us. God says this is a sin. But God forgives that sin, washes it away with Jesus' blood, like my mother washed the dirt from my jacket. His Holy Spirit gives us the power to use His name correctly.

Glad to Worship God

Remember the Sabbath day by keeping it holy.

Bible Reference: Ex. 20:8–11.

Let's pretend that you have the best aunt in all the world. Aunt Jane has always done wonderful things for you. When you were a baby, Aunt Jane waited with your parents for you to be born. When you were just a few weeks old, she held you as your sponsor at your Baptism. She bought you a beautiful christening gown and paid for the dinner in your honor.

When you were little, Aunt Jane often sent you packages with toys or new clothes, even when it wasn't your birthday. If you went to her house for a visit, she always had your favorite kind of cookies waiting for you. She let you choose what you would like to do on your visit, and she always had time to play games or read stories with you. On summer afternoons she took you to the zoo, and in winter the two of you went sledding in the park.

Last summer Aunt Jane invited you to go along with her on a trip to Disneyland. She paid for the hotel and the tickets, and she bought you every souvenir you wanted.

How would you feel about Aunt Jane if she were really your aunt? Would she be an important part of your life? Would you let her know how much you love her? Would you tell anyone about the wonderful things she had done for you?

Suppose your parents said, "We're going to Aunt Jane's house next Sunday afternoon. Would you like to go?" Would you be excited about going? Or would you make excuses, trying to think of other things you would like to do instead?

You may not have an Aunt Jane, but you do have a God who has done even more for you than this imaginary aunt. God made you and all the world you live in. He placed you in a family where you could grow up surrounded by love. He gave you rules to live by. Because you sometimes disobey Him, He sent His own Son, Jesus, to die in your place. He gives you His Holy Spirit to help you believe in Him and live the way He wants you to live. And He promises to take you to heaven to live with Him forever.

How do you feel about God and all He has done for you? Do you want to spend time with Him, to tell Him how much you love Him?

God's people spend time with Him and tell Him how much they love Him when they come together for worship. In worship they remember the things He has done, especially the life and death of Jesus. Christians love to come to God's house because of all He has done for them.

And just like you would be quick to tell your friends about your wonderful Aunt Jane, Christians can't help telling others about their wonderful God and all He has done for them.

A Family from God

Honor your father and your mother.

Bible Reference: Gen. 4:1–16.

Materials: A newspaper.

Not very long ago, several newspapers carried stories about children who went to court to divorce their parents. These children said that their home life was so terrible that they would be better off without their parents.

This certainly isn't the way God wanted family life to be. When He created the world, He blessed the living creatures He had made and told them to increase in number and fill the earth. He made Adam in His own image, then made Eve to be his wife. He planned for Adam and Eve to live together in love and have perfect children.

But Adam and Eve sinned, and their sin spoiled the perfect world God had created. The Bible tells about the family of Adam and Eve, how their sons, Cain and Abel, brought sacrifices to God. Cain, who was a farmer, brought some grain. Abel, who was a shepherd, brought a lamb. Because Abel loved God with his whole heart, he brought his finest lamb. When Cain saw that God like Abel's sacrifice better than his, he was very angry. He was so angry that some time later he killed Abel.

God saw what Cain had done. He asked Cain, "Where is your brother?"

Cain said, "I don't know. Do I always have to look out for him?"

God punished Cain. He had to leave Adam and Eve and wander for the rest of his life. But God still loved Cain. He gave him a special mark so people would not kill him. God kept Cain safe.

Even though they had sinned, God still loved Adam and Eve and their family. He gave them another son. Seth would be the ancestor of the Savior God had promised to send to take away their sin.

Sometimes our families seem as full of anger and hurt as Adam and Eve's. That's not how God intended family life to be. Our problems, like theirs, are the result of sin.

But God still loves us. He kept His promise to send the Savior. He gave His own Son, Jesus, to die on the cross to take the punishment we deserved for our sin. Because of Jesus, all of our sins are forgiven.

God gives us the power to believe in Jesus. And He gives us the power to love and obey our parents, knowing that they are forgiven sinners too. Through Jesus we can have the kind of family life that God intended for us.

Heal the Hurt
You shall not murder.

Bible Reference: Luke 10:25–37.

Materials: A well-worn Band-Aid.

I have a friend who keeps a Band-Aid like this in his wallet. *Show Band-Aid*. He says it reminds him of what obeying the Fifth Commandment means.

In the Bible Luke writes about an expert in the Law who came to Jesus with a question. "Teacher," he asked, "what must I do to inherit eternal life?"

"What is written in the Law?" Jesus asked him.

The lawyer knew the Law. "Love God and love your neighbor," he replied.

Jesus knew that the lawyer believed he had kept the Law. But Jesus knew the man had not shown love to his neighbors by caring for them. So He told the lawyer this story.

"A man on his way from Jerusalem to Jericho was attacked by robbers, who beat him and left him for dead. A priest saw the injured man, but didn't stop to help. A Levite who worked at the temple also saw him, but he passed by too.

"Finally a Samaritan saw the poor man. He bent down and poured oil and wine on the man's wounds, bandaging them with strips of cloth. Then he put the injured man on his donkey and led him to an inn, where he could care for him. The next morning he paid the innkeeper to take care of the man until he was well."

The lawyer must have squirmed when Jesus finished the story. He was sure that he, like the priest and the Levite, had not murdered anyone. But Jesus implied that they had not kept the Law if they had not done everything possible to help their neighbors in their physical need. Jesus asked the lawyer, "Which of the three was a neighbor to the man who was hurt?"

The lawyer replied, "The one who showed mercy."

Jesus told him, "Go and do likewise."

More than any neighbor, Jesus has shown mercy to us. He heals all our hurts and sicknesses—especially the sickness of the soul that is sin. Through His suffering and death He forgives us and gives us the power to live as He commands.

In love for Jesus, we obey the Fifth Commandment by doing much more than not killing our neighbors. We help people around us in all their physical needs—hurt and sickness, hunger and homelessness. We help when we let people know that we care about their needs through words of support and comfort—a card to someone who is sick, a phone call or visit to someone who is old and lonely. We help by sharing what we have—a family dinner with a neighbor who is alone, outgrown clothes or canned goods for a drive to help the homeless. We defend the child who is picked on in the classroom or on the playground.

My friend's Band-Aid is a great reminder of all we can do to be the kind of merciful neighbor Jesus wants us to be.

Respect for the Way God Made Us
You shall not commit adultery.

Bible References: Gen. 1:27–28; 2:20b–25.
Materials: A folded piece of paper.

One day a girl named Gina came home from school looking like she had lost her best friend.

"What's the matter, Gina?" her mother asked.

"I don't know, Mom," Gina tried to explain. "It's what was going on at school today. It just made me feel like dirt."

Gina pulled a tiny piece of paper from her pocket. She unfolded the paper and showed her mother the cartoon. *Unfold paper and look at it.* "The boys at school were all laughing at this. The girls wanted to see it, too, so they showed it to us. Some of the girls laughed and acted like it was funny, but it really made me feel uncomfortable."

Mother looked at the cartoon. It showed a naked woman dancing while two men watched and laughed. She folded the paper and set it on the kitchen table.

"I think I know why it made you uncomfortable, Gina," Mother said. "The cartoon makes fun of the way God made women. You know that your body is a special gift from God, not a joke. It's made the way it is so that you can be a wife and a mother when you grow up. That's part of God's wonderful plan for families."

"Then why do people make fun of the way our bodies are made?" asked Gina.

"Sin makes us belittle the gifts God gave. Cartoons like this put down men, too, making us believe that they only think of women in this way. They make us forget that God planned for men to be loving husbands and fathers. He gave boys bodies that will make them ready for the roles He planned for them.

"God has plans for adult men and women too. He wants them to respect the person who loves them, to be faithful to the person to whom they are married. He intended marriage to be a loving partnership that lasts for a lifetime."

Gina thought about what Mother had said. "Sometimes I forget about the plans God has for us. I feel bad about the times I've made fun of the way people are made."

Mother put her arm around Gina. "I'm glad we know about God's plans for us. Remember, His greatest plan was to send His Son, Jesus, to pay for our sins. We know that God forgives the wrong things we do for Jesus' sake. And He gives us the power to live as Christian boys and girls and men and women."

Gina picked up the folded paper and threw it in the waste basket. *Crumple paper and throw it away.* "We won't be needing this, will we, Mom?" she smiled. "God's plan is a whole lot better than the one in this cartoon!"

Steal No More
You shall not steal.

Bible Reference: Luke 19:1–10.

Materials: An account book or ledger.

Everyone knew Zacchaeus was a thief. Not an ordinary thief, of course, who broke into houses and stole the candlesticks, but a high-class, white-collar kind of thief. He had made his fortune as chief tax collector at Jericho—a government job that didn't pay very well but had lots of fringe benefits.

Like his fellow tax collectors, Zacchaeus knew how to work the system. When old Simon of Jericho came to pay his taxes, Zacchaeus looked in the tax book and saw that Simon owed 10 silver denarii. *Open ledger and pretend to read.* "That will be 20 denarii, Simon," Zacchaeus would say, sending 10 denarii to Rome and the other 10 into his pocket.

The people of Jericho hated Zacchaeus. They knew he charged them more than he should. And they hated the Roman government he represented.

Zacchaeus had no friends in Jericho. But he could not stop stealing from the people. Even if he would have decided to quit, no one would have believed him. Everyone knew he stole because he was a tax collector.

Then Zacchaeus met Jesus. Zacchaeus had heard people talk about this Man from Galilee who performed miracles. When he heard Jesus was coming to Jericho, short little Zacchaeus climbed a sycamore tree to get a better view.

Jesus stopped under the sycamore tree and looked up at Zacchaeus. "Zacchaeus, come down immediately," Jesus said. "I must stay at your house today."

Zacchaeus could hardly believe his ears. Jesus, who knew everything, was coming to his house! Even though he was a thief, Jesus loved him. Zacchaeus ran home joyfully.

Jesus' love and forgiveness changed Zacchaeus completely. "Look, Lord," he said, "here and now I give half of my possessions to the poor, and if I have cheated anybody out of anything, I will pay back four times the amount."

Jesus said, "Today salvation has come to this house. The Son of Man came to seek and to save what was lost."

Without Jesus, Zacchaeus could only steal. With Jesus—with His love and His forgiveness—Zacchaeus could pay back four times what he had stolen and share what he had with the poor.

Without Jesus, you and I—like Zacchaeus—cannot break the cycle of stealing. We try to get the possessions of other people for ourselves. We steal time from people for whom we should be working. We cling tightly to what we have and refuse to share with people in need.

But we have met Jesus too. We have experienced His love and forgiveness. With Jesus we have the power to repay what we have stolen and gladly share our possessions with others.

Speaking the Truth in Love
You shall not give false testimony against your neighbor.

Bible References: Matt. 26:57–68; Eph. 4:14–16.

Materials: An empty medicine bottle with blank labels on both sides; on one side, Rx prescription medicine; on the other a Mr. Yuk sticker.

If you see a bottle with a label like this, what does it mean? *Show the Rx side of the bottle.* Yes, this is the symbol for medicine. The right medicine will help to make you well when you are sick.

Turn the bottle around to show the poison label. What does this symbol mean? *Give children time to respond.* The Mr. Yuk sticker means poison. Whatever is in this bottle may make you very sick or even kill you.

But the two labels are on the same bottle. The liquid in this bottle will either heal you or hurt you. It all depends on how you use it. If you are sick and take the medicine the way the doctor prescribed, and in the amounts he told you, it should make you feel better. But if you don't need this medicine, and you decide to drink the whole bottle because it tastes like cherry juice, you may become very sick or even die.

Words are a lot like this medicine. Words can heal, or words can hurt. It all depends on how you use them.

The night before Jesus died, His enemies captured Him in the Garden and brought Him before the High Priest, Caiaphas, to be tried. Of course, Jesus had done nothing wrong. But His enemies called false witnesses to tell lies about Him. One of the witnesses said, "This Man said He is able to destroy the temple of God and rebuild it in three days."

Now this wasn't what Jesus had said at all. Once, when speaking about His own body, He said, "Destroy this temple, and I will raise it again in three days." He truthfully told what would happen to Him at His death and resurrection.

The witnesses' false words were like poison. Caiaphas and the leaders decided that Jesus must die.

But Jesus' death was all part of God's plan. God had promised Adam and Eve in the Garden of Eden that He would send a Savior to save them from their sin. Through century after century God's people had waited for that Savior to come. Jesus, God's Son, was put to death on the cross in our place, to take the punishment for our sins. Then He rose again and went back to heaven.

Jesus gives people who believe in Him the power to use words for good and not for evil. We speak the truth in love when we encourage and support each other in our troubles. Our words heal instead of hurt when we turn back anger with a kind word. Our words show Christ's love when we offer a friendly greeting to someone who needs a friend. And our words help build God's kingdom when we tell others what Jesus has done for us.

Godliness with Contentment

You shall not covet your neighbor's house.
You shall not covet your neighbor's wife, or his manservant
or maidservant, his ox or donkey, or anything that belongs
to your neighbor.

Bible References: Luke 12:13–21, 1 Tim. 6:6–10.

Materials: A Christmas catalog or other toy catalog.

One afternoon when I was visiting at a friend's house, I went downstairs to the children's playroom. Shelves of books and board games lined one entire end of the room. Next to the books stood cabinets my friend had built to hold building sets and science kits. Big toy boxes overflowed with stuffed animals. In one corner a big-screen TV was hooked up to the latest video game set, and cartridges covered the floor.

I found my friend's children sitting in the middle of the room, paging through this catalog. *Show catalog.* "If only I had this … " the daughter whined.

The son nodded sadly, "I wish we had this new toy to play with."

I stared in amazement. "But you have so many toys," I said.

The children looked around the room. "What toys?" they asked.

Their response reminded me of a story that Jesus told. A man had asked Jesus to help him get part of his inheritance away from his brother. Jesus could see the man's greed. So He replied:

"The ground of a certain rich man produced a good crop. He thought to himself, 'What shall I do? I have no place to store my crops…. I will tear down my barns and build bigger ones, and there I'll store all my grain and goods. Then I'll be set for the rest of my life. I'll eat, drink, and be merry.'

"But God said to him, 'You fool! This very night your life will be demanded from you. Then who will get what you have prepared for yourself?'"

Jesus concluded, "This is how it will be with anyone who stores up things for himself but is not rich toward God."

Like the rich fool and my friend's children, we often worry about things we would like to have. We forget the important things God has already provided: life and health, family, enough food and clothing for our needs. Most important, God has provided what only He can give: forgiveness for our sins through His Son, Jesus, and the promise of eternal life.

St. Paul wrote to young Timothy, "Godliness with contentment is great gain." Through Jesus we are given the power to be happy with what we have. Because of what He has done for us, He is more important in our lives than our possessions.

God, Our Father

Bible References: Gen. 1–3, Luke 3:21–38.

Materials: Two family-tree charts (see Appendix); scissors; cellophane tape.

I have been working on a family tree. *Show chart 1.* I put my name here at the top. On the next set of lines I wrote the names of my father and mother. Below that, I put their parents, my grandparents. I could continue this family tree for more generations, until I come to the place where I don't know the names of my ancestors.

If I could continue all the way back to creation, I would come to Adam and Eve, the people God created. They are the ancestors of all the people who have ever lived.

Luke provides this family tree of Jesus in his Gospel. *Show chart 2.* Luke uses only the names of the fathers, finally tracing Jesus' ancestors back to "Enosh, the son of Seth, the son of Adam, the son of God" (*Luke 3:38*).

We could put God on the final line of our family tree too. Since He created Adam and Eve and gave them the ability to reproduce, God is really the Father of all people, of Jesus as well as the rest of us.

Jesus often referred to God as His Father when He was here on earth. Like a Father, He provides us with everything we need. He takes care of us and protects us from harm and danger. He invites us to come to Him with our needs, and He listens to our prayers.

But Adam and Eve, the first children of God, sinned. They disobeyed God when they made the fruit they wanted to eat more important than God and His commands. Their sin separated them from God, breaking up God's family in the Garden and cutting off the human family tree from its heavenly Father. *Cut "God" off from the rest of the family tree in chart 2.*

But God still loved Adam and Eve. He promised to send a Savior to restore His lost children. After many centuries, He sent His own Son, Jesus, to suffer and die for the sins of Adam and Eve and everyone on the human family tree.

Jesus restored God's broken family. *Use tape and the strip with Jesus' name on it to reattach the rest of the family tree to God.* God didn't make us His children again because we are so smart or beautiful or because we try so hard to do what He wants. Only through faith in Jesus do we become God's children once more. Because of Jesus, our family tree now ends "sons and daughters of Enosh, the son of Seth, the son of Adam, the son of God."

Jesus, Our Redeemer

Bible Reference: John 3.

Materials: A picture of a child and dog (see Appendix).

God's Son, Jesus, came into the world to save us—to redeem us. But what does it mean to redeem someone?

I know a boy named Nathan who had always wanted a dog. He had seen exactly the dog he wanted at the pet store in the mall. Nathan's parents said he could have the dog if he bought it himself and took care of it. So Nathan, who wanted the dog very badly, raked leaves for Mr. Brown and ran errands for Mrs. Schmidt and washed his father's car and saved every penny he earned until he had enough money to pay for the dog.

Nathan and his father built a pen for the dog in the backyard. Then they went to the mall. Nathan bought the dog, some dog food, and all the things he would need to take care of his pet. It cost every cent he had earned, but Nathan loved the dog so much that he didn't mind at all.

Nathan named his dog Sparky. He fed and brushed him every day. He played with him and took him for long walks. At night he locked Sparky in his pen in the backyard.

One morning, when Nathan brought food out to Sparky's pen, he found the lock had been broken and the gate opened. Sparky was gone!

Nathan searched the entire neighborhood without finding a trace of Sparky. He made signs to hang on the telephone poles and shop windows around town. The signs had Sparky's picture and said, "Lost dog. If you find him, please call 555-1212." But no one called about the dog.

Then one day, when Nathan was walking to school, he heard a dog barking behind a fence. He stood on his tiptoes and saw that the dog was Sparky.

Nathan went up to the door of the house and rang the bell. But the owner of the house claimed the dog was his. "He's a very expensive dog," the owner said, "but he is for sale. You can buy him if you want."

Nathan knew the dog was really his. But the only way he could get Sparky back was to buy him again. So Nathan raked for Mr. Brown, ran errands for Mrs. Schmidt, washed his father's car, and saved all his money until he could buy Sparky back.

Finally Nathan brought Sparky home. "Now you're really mine," Nathan said as he hugged his dog. "First I bought you; then, when you were gone, I bought you back again."

We belonged to God because He made us. But we were separated from God by our sin. We couldn't go back to Him ourselves because sin stood in our way. But God sent Jesus to buy us back again—to redeem us. Jesus didn't buy us with money, but with His own blood, His innocent suffering and death.

Because of what Jesus, our Redeemer, did, we are bought back to God again. And because of Jesus, we will live with God forever.

The Holy Spirit

Bible Reference: Gal. 5:22–26.

Materials: Apple seeds, an apple.

Two friends were talking about Christianity. "I haven't decided yet whether I believe in Jesus or not," one said. "If I decide that I do, I'll have to work on building myself a strong faith like the other Christians I know. I'm not sure just how to go about it."

The Bible teaches that we can't come to believe in Jesus by ourselves. Faith in Jesus is the gift of the Holy Spirit.

These apple seeds remind us of faith. *Show the apple seeds.* We know that nothing will grow from the apple seeds until they are planted in the ground. But the ground can't come get the apple seeds, dig a hole, and plant them itself. Someone must bring the seeds to the ground and plant them.

The Holy Spirit plants faith in God in our hearts. The Spirit works through the Gospel, the Good News that Jesus died to take away our sins. When we hear the Good News in God's Word, the Holy Spirit makes us able to believe that Jesus died for us.

Apple seeds planted in the ground begin to grow. First a tiny plant sprouts from the soil. Then, as rain falls and sun warms the little leaves, the plant grows into a mighty tree.

The Holy Spirit nourishes the faith He has planted in our hearts. Faith grows as we learn more about God and what He has done for us. The Spirit helps us grow through Bible study, through hearing God's Word in church, Sunday school, and other church classes.

As an apple tree grows, we have one sure way of knowing that it's really an apple tree— it bears apples! *Show the apple.* Christians, too, are known by their fruit. St. Paul wrote to the Christians in Galatia, "The fruit of the Spirit is love, joy, peace, patience, kindness, goodness, faithfulness, gentleness, and self-control."

We can't bear fruit like that on our own. Our sinfulness will always bring the opposite fruit: hatred, unhappiness, anger, impatience, meanness, jealousy, greed, selfish ambition, fits of rage. But God has forgiven our sins for Jesus' sake. And He gives us the Holy Spirit to help us bear good fruit for Him. Through the work of the Holy Spirit we can serve each other in love, the way God planned.

The Holy Spirit doesn't work only in your heart and mine; He works in the hearts of all who believe in Jesus. Together He makes us into the Christian church, in which we worship God and support one another in our faith. The Holy Spirit keeps that church with Jesus until it becomes His triumphant church in heaven.

The Holy Spirit gives us the power to tell others about our Savior, Jesus. In this way He works through us to plant the seed of faith in the hearts of new believers.

Dad, I Need to Talk to You
Our Father, who art in heaven.

Bible Reference: Luke 11:1–13.

Materials: Picture of a father with children (see Appendix).

Fathers. Sometimes they're busy, working late or doing chores around the house. Sometimes they're in a hurry, rushing to be on time for work or a meeting at church. And sometimes they're tired after a long day on the job or in the yard or helping care for children. But most of the time, when you need to talk to them, they will listen.

Fathers listen to their children for several reasons. They love their children. They know their children make mistakes, but they love them enough to forgive them and help them try again. They know their children need them and depend on them for help. When children want to talk to their father, the father feels their love for him.

Jesus teaches us to talk to our heavenly Father. This Father is the God who created the universe. His mighty power overwhelms us, because we know we don't deserve to come and talk to Him. But we know that Jesus died to make us God's children. For Jesus' sake God has forgiven all of our sins. Because of Jesus we can talk to God as our Father, knowing that He will listen.

Our heavenly Father wants us to talk to Him because He loves and forgives us. He knows that we can do nothing by ourselves. He wants us to depend on Him for all that we need. When we come to talk to Him as His children, our heavenly Father knows that we love Him.

Jesus promises us, "Ask and it will be given to you; seek and you will find; knock and the door will be opened to you. For everyone who asks receives; he who seeks finds; and to him who knocks, the door will be opened" (*Luke 11:9–10*).

Unlike earthly fathers who may be busy or tired, God is always ready to hear our prayers. Jesus says, "Which of you fathers, if your son asks for a fish, will give him a snake instead? Or if he asks for an egg, will give him a scorpion? If you then, though you are evil, know how to give good gifts to your children, how much more will your Father in heaven give the Holy Spirit to those who ask Him!" (*Luke 11:11–13*).

The Holy Spirit, who puts faith in Jesus in our hearts and makes it grow, helps us come to our heavenly Father in prayer. He teaches us the words to say. He gives us the power to believe that God hears and answers our prayers.

Three Cheers for God
Hallowed be Thy name.

Bible Reference: Is. 6:1–8.

Materials: A megaphone or cheerleader's pom-poms.

Have you ever attended a football or basketball game? Whom did you see at the game that would use something like this? How did they use it? *Show the megaphone or pom-poms and encourage the children to describe the actions of the cheerleaders.* Why do sports teams and fans like to have cheerleaders at their games?

Cheerleaders keep the fans at a game excited. They tell the fans how good the team is. They point out all the wonderful things the team does. They help the fans support the team by yelling together. When the cheerleaders shout, "Two bits, four bits, six bits, a dollar—all for Mayville stand up and holler!" the Mayville fans will all jump up and yell to show how much they love their team. Another cheer, "Dribble left, dribble right, we've got a team that will fight, fight fight!" reminds people how well their team has fought in other games. Or a cheer might praise the efforts of an individual player: "Jerry, Jerry, he's our man—if he can't do it, no one can!"

Long before Jesus was born, God gave the prophet Isaiah a vision of heaven. In this vision Isaiah saw God sitting on His throne. Above Him were six-winged angels who called to one another, "Holy, holy, holy is the LORD Almighty; the whole earth is full of His glory." The sound of their voices shook the doors of heaven and filled the temple with smoke.

Terror filled Isaiah, who knew he was a sinner and didn't deserve to stand in the presence of God. "Woe to me," cried Isaiah, "for I am a man of unclean lips."

Then one of the angels took a fiery coal from the altar and touched Isaiah's lips. "See," the angel said, "this has touched your lips. Your guilt is taken away, and your sin is paid for."

Wouldn't you love to have been there to hear those heavenly cheerleaders and join their shouts of praise to the Father, Son, and Holy Spirit? You might feel afraid at first, like Isaiah did, because of your sin. But your guilt has been taken away, too, and your sins paid for when Jesus died for you on the cross.

Because we have been forgiven, we can join the angels, praising God's holy name. We praise Him together when we gather for worship in our churches and Bible school classes. We praise Him with our families when we have family devotions. And we praise Him by ourselves when we talk to Him in prayer.

After the angel had touched his lips, Isaiah heard God say, "Whom shall I send? And who will go for us?"

Isaiah answered, "Here I am. Send me!"

Forgiven and full of praise, Isaiah was ready to share God's holy name with others. Forgiven and praise-filled, we share His name by telling others what He has done for us.

Stories of the Kingdom
Thy kingdom come.

Bible Reference: Matthew 13.

Materials: A copy of Aesop's fables.

Have you ever heard the story of the boy who cried wolf? Or the tale of the crow who dropped stones into the water jug until the water was high enough for him to drink? Do you know the fable about the greedy animal who saw his reflection in the water and dropped the food in his own mouth while trying to grab his reflection's food?

All of these fables are credited to an ancient person from Greece named Aesop. He told each of these stories to teach a lesson—about lying or cleverness or greed. The people who heard Aesop's stories understood the lessons because the stories were about people or animals they knew very well.

Jesus told stories about everyday people and situations too. The people who listened understood what Jesus was talking about and learned from the lessons He taught. Jesus' stories are called parables, and they are recorded in the Gospels.

Many of Jesus' parables told about the kingdom of God. People learned what it was like to be part of God's kingdom on earth. They learned the importance of God's kingdom. They learned that the kingdom of God would last forever, and that they could live in God's kingdom in heaven.

"The kingdom of God," said Jesus, "is like a man who sowed good seed in his field. At night an enemy sowed weeds in the same field. The wheat and weeds grew up together. But at the harvest, the farmer burned the weeds and carried the good wheat home to his barn." Jesus meant that believers and unbelievers live side by side in the world. But at the end of the world, He will come to take the believers home with Him to heaven.

Jesus said, "The kingdom of heaven is like yeast that a woman mixes into her bread dough. The little bit of yeast works all through the dough." Jesus meant that the Holy Spirit works through believers to bring faith in the Gospel to the people around them.

"The kingdom of heaven is like a treasure hidden in a field," said Jesus. "When a man found it, he hid it again. Then in his joy he sold all that he had and bought the field." Jesus meant that the kingdom is of such great value that we should be willing to give up all that we have to be a part of it.

When we pray, "Thy kingdom come," we ask that God, through His grace in Jesus, will make us a part of His kingdom here on earth. As forgiven members of this kingdom, He gives us the power to live as His children. He will help us spread His Word to people who have not heard the Good News of salvation. And we pray that the Holy Spirit will keep us in faith so that we will be a part of His glorious kingdom in heaven.

God's Way

Thy will be done on earth as it is in heaven.

Bible Reference: Matt. 26:36–46.

Materials: A mixing bowl and wire whip.

My friend John can cook anything. He works as head chef in a restaurant, preparing meals for hundreds of people every day. He shows the other cooks in the restaurant the correct way to prepare fancy dishes with French names. I wish I could cook like John.

I'm learning to be a better cook. Some things I learn from reading cookbooks or watching television shows about cooking. But my best lessons come from my friend, John. Whenever I go to his house for dinner, I watch him very carefully. *Show bowl and wire whip.* I pay attention to which bowls or pans or utensils he uses. I note which ingredients he chooses for each dish he prepares. I'm becoming a better cook by following John's example.

Children learn to do many things by following their parents' example—things like washing the car or making sandwiches or swinging a baseball bat. A good example leads to learning good skills; a bad example may bring bad habits that are hard to break.

Jesus taught His disciples how to pray. He taught them to say, "Thy will be done on earth as it is in heaven." Then He gave them an example to follow.

On the night before He died, Jesus took His disciples to a garden to pray. He knew that He would die for the sins of all people the next day. He knew that people would lie about Him to judges who didn't care about the truth. He knew that the nails and thorns would hurt terribly. He knew He would be left to die all alone. So Jesus prayed to His heavenly Father. Three times He pleaded, "Is there any other way?" But Jesus also knew that God's plan to take away our sins made it necessary for Him to die on the cross. So He prayed, "Yet not as I will, but as You will."

The heavenly Father heard Jesus' prayer. He sent an angel to comfort Jesus. He made Him strong enough to do His Father's will. When Jesus finished praying, He was ready to do everything His Father had planned for Him to do—even die on the cross for us.

We follow the example of Jesus' prayer when we pray, "Thy will be done on earth as it is in heaven." We ask God to answer our prayers by doing what He knows is best for us. We pray that He would show us what He wants us to do. We ask Him to help us always remember that what He wants for us is best because He loves us so much.

Trusting God for Bread
Give us this day our daily bread.

Bible Reference: Exodus 16.

Materials: A slice of bread.

When Jesus taught His disciples to pray, He told them to say, "Give us this day our daily bread." *Show bread.* The idea of just enough bread for each day may have sounded familiar to the disciples. It may have reminded them of what God did for their ancestors in the desert so many centuries before.

Moses and his brother, Aaron, had led the people of Israel out of Egypt. God had parted the waters of the Red Sea so that they could cross safely, but the Egyptian army following them drowned. God had come to them on Mount Sinai and given them His Law. Now they were crossing the desert to return to their homeland.

But deserts don't have enough food and water for millions of people on their way home. Soon the people of Israel grew hungry. They grumbled and complained to Moses and Aaron. They said they wished they had stayed in Egypt, where there was plenty of good food.

God heard the people's grumbling. He told Moses, "Tell the people I will give them food. Every evening they will eat meat, and every morning they will be filled with bread. Then they will know that I am God."

That same evening quail came and covered the camp. The people cooked the quail and ate them. In the morning thin, white flakes appeared like frost on the desert. When the Israelites saw it, they said, "What is it?"

Moses said, "It's the bread God said He would send. Take only enough for one day; don't keep any for tomorrow."

The people gathered bread for their families. Some people worried that God wouldn't send more bread, so they took enough to save for the next day. In the morning their bread was full of maggots and smelled awful.

The people called the bread *manna,* which means, "What is it?" For 40 years God provided manna every morning and quail every evening. The people of Israel didn't need any other food.

We know that God provides everything that we need—food, clothing, a place to live, a job for support, a family to care for us. But, like the people of Israel, we often worry. What if I lose my job? What if I get sick? What if we don't have enough money for college or a nice vacation or a bigger house or a new car?

When we pray, "Give us this day our daily bread," we thank God for providing all that we need. We acknowledge that all good gifts come from Him. We ask Him to forgive us for not trusting Him and for worrying about how we will get the things we think we need. We pray that God will help us to be content with what we have and to share what He has given us with others.

As You Have Been Forgiven

Forgive us our trespasses as we forgive those who trespass against us.

Bible Reference: Matt. 18:21–35.

Materials: Two cloth pouches, or sandwich bags, one stuffed with coins and the other containing only a few.

When Jesus taught His disciples to pray, He told them to say, "Forgive us our trespasses as we forgive those who trespass against us."

The disciples often wondered about forgiving other people. One day Peter asked Jesus, "How many times do I have to forgive my brother? Is seven times enough?"

Jesus answered, "Not seven times, but seventy times seven." He meant that we should always forgive each other, the way God forgives us. Then He told Peter this story.

"The kingdom of heaven is like a king who wanted to settle accounts with his servants. First he called a servant who owed him 10,000 talents. *Show the bag stuffed with coins*. The servant didn't have enough money to pay the king what he owed him. So the king ordered that the servant and his whole family be sold into slavery.

"The servant fell on his knees in front of the king and begged, 'Be patient with me, and I will pay back everything.' The king felt sorry for his servant and canceled the debt. Now the servant owed him nothing.

"But that same servant went out and found another servant who owed him only a small amount of money. *Show the bag with just a few coins*. He grabbed him and began to choke him. 'Pay me what you owe me!' he demanded.

"'Be patient with me, and I will pay you back,' pleaded the servant.

"But the first servant refused. He had his fellow servant thrown into prison until he could pay the debt. When the other servants saw what had happened, they told the king.

"The king called for the first servant. 'You wicked man,' the king said. 'I forgave all that you owed me. Shouldn't you have done the same for your fellow servant?' Then the king had the unforgiving servant thrown in jail.

"This is how my heavenly Father will treat each of you unless you forgive each other from your heart," Jesus concluded.

Our sins against God make us look like the first servant. We have lied, cheated, disobeyed, taken things that don't belong to us, hurt each other with our words and actions, misused God's name, and failed to worship Him. We have not kept God most important in our lives. Yet God forgives us. He gave His only Son, Jesus, to take the punishment for our sins.

God wants us to follow His example and to forgive other people when they sin against us. Through Jesus He gives us the power to love and forgive people who hurt us, just as He forgives us.

Will the Real Devil Please Stand Up?
And lead us not into temptation.

Bible Reference: Matt. 4:1–11.

Materials: Three sheets of paper, numbered 1, 2, and 3.

Long ago I often watched a TV show called "To Tell the Truth." Each week a contestant listened to the stories of three people who all claimed to have the same name. The contestant could ask each person several questions. Then he had to decide which guest, number 1, 2, or 3, was the person he said he was. *Show the number cards.* After the contestant guessed, the host would say, "Will the real Mr. Jones please stand up?" Only the person who had been telling the truth would stand.

Let's do an imaginary show. We'll pretend that the special guest is that old tempter, the devil. You, as the contestant, will have to guess which guest is really the devil. And we'll make this game a little different than the old TV show. Each person will try and convince you that he or she is not the devil.

Hold up card with number 1. Guest 1 says, "I'm not really the devil. You know me. I'm your friend, Jeff, who lives next door. Remember me? I was the one who convinced you to stay outside and play a little longer after your mother called you for supper. She just wanted to spoil all your fun. Anyway, you're getting too old to have to do everything she says. I'm not the devil; I'm just Jeff."

Hold up card 2. Guest 2 has a similar story. "The devil? Not me! I'm Susan, the girl who sits next to you in school. Remember? I put my spelling paper way out on the edge of my desk so you could see the words that day when you had forgotten to study. I'm a real friend— I helped you when you needed help. The devil wouldn't do that for you."

Hold up card 3. Guest 3 wears a black leather jacket and looks strangely familiar. "I'm not the devil, although he's a pretty cool dude too. I'm the baddest kid in your whole neighborhood. I hang out down on the corner, and I've got drugs that will make you cool, like me. Stop by and see me sometime. I'll even let you try some for free. Would the devil do that for you?"

How will you decide which one of these contestants is the devil? Isn't he supposed to wear a red suit and carry a pitchfork so you'll recognize him?

You take a guess. Finally the host asks the question, "Will the real devil please stand up?" All three guests stand up!

The hardest part of recognizing the devil when he tempts us to sin is that he looks so much like our friends.

When we pray, "And lead us not into temptation," we ask God to help us recognize when the devil, through people or even our own selves, is tempting us to disobey God. We ask God to forgive the times we have given in to that temptation. And we pray for strength to say no to the devil, whatever he looks like.

God, Our Savior
But deliver us from evil.

Bible Reference: Daniel 3.

Materials: A life preserver.

In a life full of danger, it's great to know someone is around to save you. For a swimmer or a passenger on a boat, that savior might be a person with a life preserver. *Show life preserver.* When the rescuer sees you are in trouble, he will throw the life preserver to you. You can stay afloat by holding on to it. He can use the rope attached to the life preserver to pull you out of danger to safety.

Three men long ago found they had a special life preserver. Shadrach, Meshach, and Abednego had been taken from Jerusalem to work for the king of Babylon. Even in Babylon they never forgot their God.

One day the king told his workers to make a statue of gold. He told the people, "This is my god. When you hear music, you must pray to my god, or you will be thrown into a hot, burning furnace."

The music played. All of the people bowed down to the king's god—all except Shadrach, Meshach, and Abednego.

The king's servants told him what had happened. He called for the three men. "If you don't pray to my god, I'll burn you in the furnace," the king threatened. "Do you think your God can save you from the fire?"

Shadrach, Meshach, and Abednego said, "Our God can save us. We will not pray to your idol."

The king told his workers to make the fire seven times hotter. Then he had them tie up the three men and throw them into the furnace. The fire burned so hot that it killed the men who threw them in.

A little while later the king looked into the furnace. "What happened?" he shouted. "Didn't we throw three men into the furnace? Now I see four, and one of them looks like an angel. They're walking in the fire, and they're not hurt one bit!"

Then the king called into the furnace, "You servants of God, come out!" Shadrach, Meshach, and Abednego walked out of the fire. Not one hair of their heads was burned. They didn't even smell like smoke.

"Praise your God!" the king said. "He sent His angel to save you. There is no god as great as your God."

We ask God to deliver us from evil because we know that He is powerful enough to save us from any trouble. He has proven that by saving us from the greatest trouble of all—sin. He did this by sending Jesus, our Savior, to die on the cross for us. And He will finally save us from all of earth's evils by taking us home to live with Him forever in the safety of heaven.

Belonging to Jesus

Bible Reference: Gal. 3:26–29.

Materials: A toy or lunch sack or other possession that you have marked with your initials.

How do you mark something that belongs to you so that you can always identify it as your own? *Allow the children to respond.*

When I want to mark something as my own, I write my initials on it. *Show toy or whatever you have brought.* If someone borrows this toy, or if it gets mixed up with toys that belong to other people, I'll always be able to find these initials and know that this toy belongs to me.

Baptism marks us as belonging to Jesus. When a person is baptized, the pastor makes the sign of the cross over his forehead and his heart to mark him as someone who was saved by Jesus when He died on the cross. The sign of the cross is like Jesus' initials.

When I write my initials on things that belong to me, I make sure I use a permanent marker. I don't want anything to remove my initials or blur them so they can't be read.

Baptism uses the most permanent mark of all. The pastor baptizes us with water. Normally markers or paints that are made with water are not permanent. But the water of Baptism is connected with God's Word and used in the way that God commanded. Before He went back to heaven, Jesus told His disciples, "Therefore go and make disciples of all nations, baptizing them in the name of the Father and of the Son and of the Holy Spirit" (*Matt. 28:19*). Water used with God's Word marks us as His forever.

When we belong to Jesus through Baptism, we share in all the things He has done. Jesus died on the cross for us. Now we don't have to die as the punishment for our own sins. Jesus came alive again on Easter. Now, through Baptism, we have a new life with Him, a life in which He gives us the power to believe in Him and live the way He wants us to live. Jesus went back to heaven to live with His heavenly Father. Someday we will go to heaven to live with Him forever.

Even though we have been baptized, we continue to sin. But because of Jesus' mark on us, we can come to God and tell Him we are sorry. We know that He will forgive us because we belong to Jesus. God's Holy Spirit helps us remember our Baptism and live for Jesus.

Someday we will stand in heaven next to our Friend, Jesus, still belonging to Him through Baptism. We know that our heavenly Father will welcome us home. Because we have been baptized, we can point to Jesus and say, "I'm His."

God's Loving Touch

Bible Reference: Matt. 26:17–30.

Jamie had been sick for a long time. Because of his illness, his body could not fight against infections. Even the germs that give us colds or the flu would kill Jamie.

Jamie's doctors wanted to protect him from all kinds of germs. So they had him moved into a special isolation bubble. In the bubble Jamie's environment was carefully controlled. The air was constantly purified, and everything that he touched had been disinfected. Nurses passed his food trays and medicine through a large plastic tube. After they had been sterilized, his toys and books could be passed through the tube too.

Jamie could see the doctors and nurses and his parents through the plastic bubble, but he could not touch them. They could talk to each other through special microphones. His friends at school couldn't visit him, but they wrote him letters that were sterilized and passed through the tube.

Inside the bubble Jamie had all the things he needed. He knew the doctors and nurses were doing everything to help him. He knew his parents loved him and his friends at school missed him. He had plenty of toys and books and could watch television through the plastic bubble. But Jamie grew sadder and sadder.

Finally the doctors decided that Jamie could leave the bubble. As soon as he was released, he hugged his mother and father. "When I was in the bubble, I knew that you loved me," Jamie explained, "but I needed to touch you to really feel your love."

We can read about God's love in the Bible and hear about it in church and Sunday school. We know that God loves us. But God understands that human beings can feel love best in things they can touch, taste, and see. That's why He gave us Holy Communion.

On the night before He died, Jesus had dinner with His disciples in Jerusalem. After they had eaten, He took bread and blessed it. He gave it to His disciples and said, "Take and eat; this is My body." Then He took a cup of wine, gave thanks, and passed it to them. "Drink from it, all of you," He said. "This is My blood of the covenant, which is poured out for many for the forgiveness of sins."

Jesus told His disciples to celebrate this special meal often to remember Him. Today Christians all over the world eat Jesus' body and drink His blood as they receive the bread and wine at Communion and remember all that their Lord did for them. They receive forgiveness of sins through this Sacrament.

Young children do not usually receive the Lord's Supper along with their parents and older brothers and sisters. People must be old enough to understand how important God's special touch in the supper is. They must be able to confess their sins and come to Holy Communion ready to receive God's forgiveness.

But children can be sure that they, too, are forgiven through Jesus' death on the cross. They can look forward to the day when they will feel God's touch in Holy Communion.

Pattern for happy/sad face paper plate, "A Bad Day That Was Good"

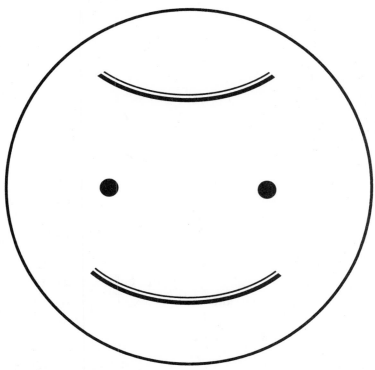

Figures for "What Shape Is Love?"

Copy, enlarge, and cut out figures.

Directions for making a cross from a palm leaf for "God's Ending"

Palm leaves can be purchased at a florist shop. Use a single palm leaf, ½″ to ¾″ wide and 36″ long for each cross. Leaves must be flexible—wrap in wet towels and refrigerate to keep them fresh.

1. Hold the leaf in a vertical position, with the edges curving toward you and the point up. About 6″ up from the base, fold back.

2. About 2 ½″ from the first fold, bend leaf to the left.

3. Bring leaf around and across the front of the vertical post, leaving end pointing to the right.

4. Wrap leaf around the vertical post again, leaving end pointing to the right.

5. About 3″ to the right of the vertical post, fold leaf forward, bringing end to the left in front of the post.

6. About 2 ½″ left of the post edge, fold back right to the front of the post.

7. At center of post, fold up.

8. Fold back and down, tucking end through loop in front of vertical post.

9. Bring end up, fold back and down through loop again. Trim ends even at the bottom.

Picture for "What Makes a Good Shepherd Good?" and "Jesus, Our Redeemer"

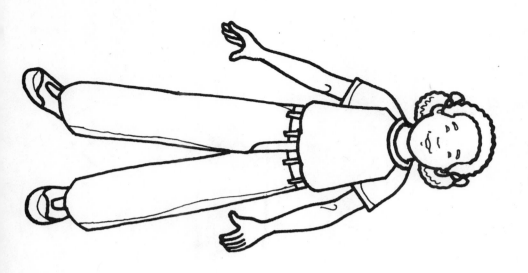

fold here

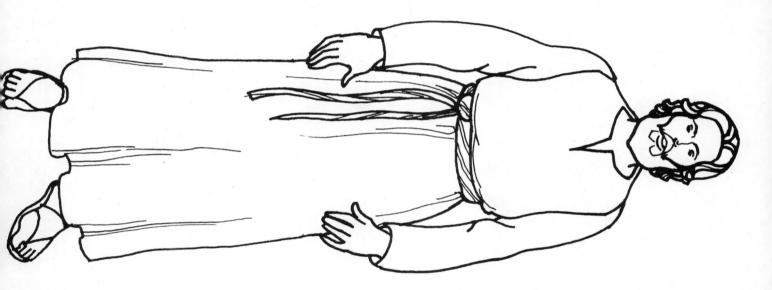

fold here

Folding picture for "Up, Up, but Not Away"

Trinity pinwheel for "A Picture of God"

Enlarge pattern and reproduce on heavy paper or cardboard. Put nail through center hole and fasten to wooden dowel like a pinwheel.

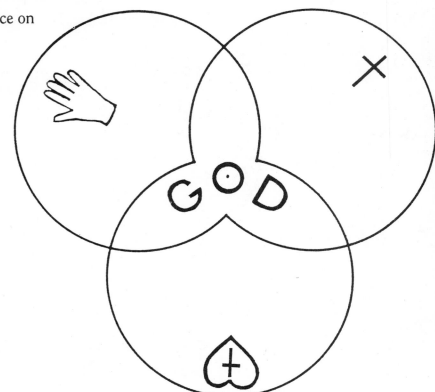

Notes for "Every Day Is Mother's Day"

I'm sorry for the things I said, Please forgive me. Aren't you glad Jesus forgives us too?

p.s. I love you.

I'm sorry for the things I said. Please forgive me. Aren't you glad Jesus forgives us too?
P.S.
I love you.

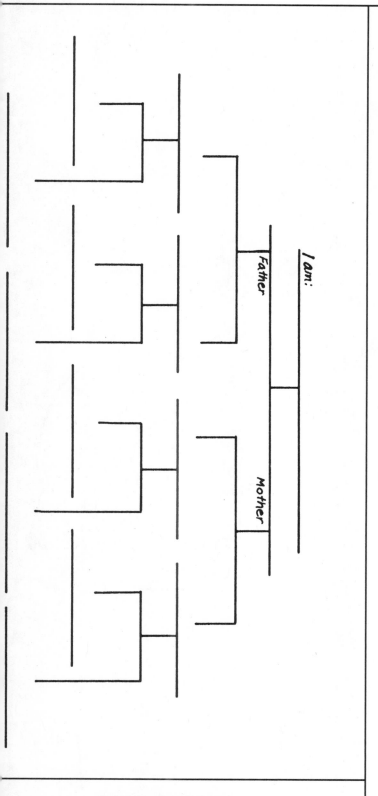

Father

Mother

I am:

JESUS

Jesus

the Son, so it was thought, of Joseph,

the son of Heli,

the son of Matthat,

the son of Levi,

the son of Melki,

the son of Janna, ...

the son of Nathan,

the son of David,

the son of Jesse,

the son of Obed,

the son of Boaz, ...

the son of Judah,

the son of Jacob,

the son of Isaac,

the son of Abraham, ...

the son of Enosh,

the son of Seth,

the son of Adam,

the son of God.

Picture for "Dad, I Need to Talk to You"